REVITALIZING RURAL ECONOMIES

Revitalizing Rural Economies

A Guide for Practitioners

YOLANDE E. CHAN, JEFFREY A. DIXON, AND
CHRISTINE R. DUKELOW

McGill-Queen's University Press
Montreal & Kingston · London · Ithaca

© McGill-Queen's University Press 2013

ISBN 978-0-7735-4213-6 (cloth)
ISBN 978-0-7735-4214-3 (paper)
ISBN 978-0-7735-8927-8 (ePDF)
ISBN 978-0-7735-8928-5 (ePUB)

Legal deposit fourth quarter 2013
Bibliothèque nationale du Québec

Printed in Canada on acid-free paper that is 100% ancient forest free
(100% post-consumer recycled), processed chlorine free

McGill-Queen's University Press acknowledges the support of the
Canada Council for the Arts for our publishing program. We also
acknowledge the financial support of the Government of Canada
through the Canada Book Fund for our publishing activities.

Library and Archives Canada Cataloguing in Publication

Chan, Yolande E., author
    Revitalizing rural economies : a guide for practitioners / Yolande E.
Chan, Jeffrey A. Dixon, and Christine R. Dukelow.

Includes bibliographical references and index.
Issued in print and electronic formats.
ISBN 978-0-7735-4213-6 (bound). – ISBN 978-0-7735-4214-3 (pbk.)
ISBN 978-0-7735-8927-8 (ePDF). – ISBN 978-0-7735-8928-5 (ePUB)

    1. Rural development – Canada – Case studies. 2. Cities and
towns – Canada – Growth – Case studies. 3. Canada – Rural
conditions – Case studies. 4. Canada – Economic conditions – Case
studies. I. Dixon, Jeffrey A., 1977–, author II. Dukelow, Christine
R., 1949–, author III. Title.

HN110.Z9C6 2013C   307.1'4120971   C2013-905255-0
                                             C2013-905256-9

Typeset by Jay Tee Graphics Ltd. in 10.5/13 Sabon

Contents

Foreword

The university has an important role to play in regional economic development[1] and should serve as a key partner in the local knowledge economy. While much university research and teaching is not applied or linked to local communities, other research conducted by faculty and students results in innovative, commercial products and processes. Students in service learning and other project-based courses apply newly gained knowledge in community settings. University members benefit as do community representatives.

Today's leading-edge universities view economic development as a key component of their mandate. They do not see this as a domain only for community colleges and other tertiary institutions. They recognize that high-quality knowledge discovery – in research and teaching – is often best conducted while looking for novel solutions to real, complex issues. Partnering with local industry, non-profits, and the government is often a good way for university representatives to identify and study issues of international, national, regional, and local significance. The knowledge gained in these research and teaching partnerships can be effectively translated and disseminated to community members who stand to gain most from its use.

University innovation parks, outreach centres, incubators, commercialization centres, technology transfer offices, and new venture and entrepreneurship programs are standard features of universities that are making an economic difference to the communities in which they are located.[2] The Monieson Centre at Queen's School of Business, Queen's University is a research centre that serves as a bridge between academics and research users outside the university. It focuses on community-university partnerships in the conduct of research that is of mutual benefit. The goal is to facilitate research of the very highest quality (resulting in top-tier journal publications and books) that has a major impact on individuals, organizations, industries and communities. Faculty and students across Queen's University and at other institutions in Canada and around the globe collaborate with community and business representatives to address complex challenges related to knowledge-based organizations and the knowledge economy.

It is in this context that the centre was pleased to help birth, in 2007, the Knowledge Impact in Society (KIS) project, funded by the Social Sciences and Humanities Research Council of Canada that created the knowledge products described in this book. The KIS project, "Revitalizing Rural Economies by Mobilizing Academic Knowledge," was designed to maximize the impact of the academy on the region. Its particular focus was initially eastern Ontario. Later projects extended its reach across southwestern Ontario, Canada, and beyond, resulting in more than $2 million of community-based research activity as of spring 2013.

I invite you to read and use this book as fully as you can. Our goal is impact – adding value and serving communities and society in the course of conducting university research. I hope that you benefit greatly.

Yolande E. Chan, PhD
Professor and Former Director, The Monieson Centre
Queen's School of Business, Queen's University
http://business.queensu.ca

Preface

Canada's economy is built in large part on its rural character. Intertwining lakes and rivers, vast, sprawling plains, towering mountains, and a wealth of natural resources provided the foundation upon which the Canadian economy was first built. While Canada's global reputation continues to be tied to its natural resources, its social fabric has changed. Through industrialization, globalization, and now digitalization, Canada has become increasingly urban-centric. Canada of the twenty-first century is a network of thriving cities with growing, diverse populations. Small towns are becoming increasingly urbanized, acting as satellite communities for nearby metropolitan centres that offer opportunities for employment, education, residence and recreation. As their role in Canadian life changes, rural communities are seeking economic revitalization. This book offers economic developers strategies for renewing rural economies.

THE CHALLENGE FOR RURAL COMMUNITIES

The economic change in Canada's rural and remote communities has been dramatic. With every new census, rural Canada's place in the national fabric unravels a bit more.[3] Low population density leads to a lack of critical mass for services and infrastructure. This leads to reduced business creation, youth out-migration, lower incomes, a smaller tax base to pay for regional and government services delivered over long distances, and fewer educational, cultural, and recreational opportunities as compared with urban areas. Demographic changes relating to an aging population and, in some communities, the in-migration of retirees add further complexity. In

> "Community Success [does] not come from size or opportunity alone, but from meeting challenges and adversity, seizing and maximizing possibilities, and developing a collection of creative solutions to apparently insoluble problems."
>
> Mike Harcourt – former premier of British Columbia
> *From Restless Communities to Resilient Places: Building a Stronger Future for All Canadians*

a growing number of areas, the economic gap created by the shrinking industrial base is being filled by small and medium-sized enterprises (SMEs) started by entrepreneurs who create new opportunities for skilled workers.

This new rural reality poses a challenge to economic development practitioners, municipalities and agencies whose role it is to build a solid economic foundation for rural communities. In the past, the focus was on traditional sources of rural economic competitiveness – natural resources and relatively low costs of production. Over the past twenty years, however, the forces of global competition, including reduced trade barriers and declining transportation costs, have eroded these advantages. New approaches and creative solutions emerging throughout the rural landscape bring opportunities for revitalizing the economic competitiveness and social well-being of many communities. Economic development practitioners, who understand better the complexity of the challenges and the critical elements of new opportunities, increase significantly their ability to create positive changes at the community level and with government policy leaders. Documenting these successes and sharing the approaches more broadly across communities is a critical element in the revitalization of rural communities across Canada and beyond.

INTRODUCTION TO THE GUIDE

Revitalizing Rural Economies: A Guide for Practitioners was developed to assist those who work to make a difference in their local and regional economies: community economic development professionals and other community leaders. The guide is the product of a collaborative partnership between Dr Yolande Chan, former director, the Monieson Centre at Queen's School of Business, Jeff Dixon, associate director, the Monieson Centre, and Christine Dukelow, an independent rural development consultant. Their knowledge and experience have been combined with the expansive base of community data emerging from the Knowledge Impact in Society (KIS) project coordinated by the centre to create a guide to support rural community economic development practitioners.

Founded in 1998, the Monieson Centre at Queen's School of Business brings leading academic research to business, government, and community audiences to create value through knowledge. The Centre focuses on research themes related to the knowledge economy – how to harness the expertise of individuals, organizations, and communities to create *knowledge capital* – integrating both theory and practice. The result is innovation, insight, and understanding to grow business, inform policy, and revitalize industries and communities. Established through generous funding from Melvin R. Goodes (former chairman and CEO of Warner-Lambert), the Centre is named in honour of the late Dr Danny Monieson. Renowned for inspirational teaching and leadership at Queen's School of Business, Danny's research focused on "usable knowledge."

Queen's School of Business (QSB) is one of Canada's premier business schools, consistently capturing top international rankings for its programs. The world-class reputation of this small, elite school is a testament to the high quality of its programs, its faculty and its students who come from Canada and abroad. Founded in 1937, the school continues to innovate as it aims to ensure that academic excellence and exceptional experience are the hallmarks of every Queen's program.

Revitalizing Rural Economies: A Guide for Practitioners is a self-help tool for economic development practitioners and other professionals at the forefront of leading change in their communities. It offers insights into the nature of the challenges facing rural communities along with real-world examples and case studies drawn from the Knowledge Impact in Society project. The book draws on a knowledge base developed collaboratively by communities, businesses, and academics, documenting the principles and practices of twenty-first century rural economic development.

The book is organized into four distinct parts. Part One, Understanding Community Economic Development – New Roles for Practitioners provides a background and context for the evolution of the

The KIS Approach

Increasingly, universities are partnering with communities to support regional economic development. They are actively mobilizing knowledge across and beyond the academy, investing in technology transfer offices, creating programs to foster new ventures and entrepreneurship, and promoting student learning via involvement in community projects. Research indicates that networks between universities and communities are a vital aspect of a thriving, innovative, entrepreneurial culture and business environment.[*]

In April 2008, the Monieson Centre at Queen's School of Business launched the Knowledge Impact in Society (KIS) project, a three-year knowledge mobilization initiative funded by the Social Sciences and Humanities Research Council of Canada (SSHRC). The project brought together academics and community leaders to address eastern Ontario's economic challenges. The partnership produced community workshops, case studies documenting business successes, syntheses of literature relevant to rural communities, social media (e.g., Facebook and Twitter), and a website (http://www.easternontarioknowledge.ca) with free resources including tools directly targeted at economic developers, policymakers, and business people.

The KIS model drew on the strengths of both academic and community partners. The project's research team consisted of three business school researchers with expertise in knowledge management, organizational behaviour, and systems analysis, a researcher in family medicine who studies healthcare service delivery, two geographers who examine creative economy innovations and environmental sustainability, two rural economic development personnel, and a business school communications specialist.

Dr Yolande Chan, then director of the Monieson Centre, was the project's principal investigator. Jeff Dixon, associate director, the Monieson Centre, served as project coordinator. The project initiatives were developed and implemented in coordination with the Prince Edward/Lennox & Addington Community Futures Development Corporation (PELA CFDC), the Eastern Ontario CFDC Network, Inc., and more than thirty supporting partners. This partnership network included provincial and national agencies concerned with rural economic development such as Industry Canada, FedNor, the Rural Secretariat, the Ontario Ministry of Agriculture, Food and Rural Affairs, the Ontario Rural Council, and the Ontario East Economic Development Commission, as well as numerous local agencies. Economic development tools and resources developed through the project achieved both increased relevancy and reach, as compared with traditional research products developed outside of community partnerships.

By 2012, the partnership had grown to over forty organizations, and benefited from more than $1,700,000 in funds to conduct collaborative, community-based research. The KIS project is an example of a leading-edge approach to mobilizing knowledge through university–community partnerships.

* Diane Palmintera, Robert Hodgson, Louis Tornatzky, Echo Xiao Xiang Lin, *Accelerating Economic Development through University Technology Transfer*, report to the Connecticut Technology Transfer and Commercialization Advisory Board of the Governor's Competitiveness Council, Innovation Associates Inc., October 2004.

art and practice of community economic development. It demonstrates how communities – both at the individual and regional levels – can leverage local assets and culture to drive economic growth. Community economic development (CED) practitioners and other community leaders will further learn how to support three key building blocks of the CED process – innovation, community assets, and vibrant downtowns. Guidelines and approaches are offered to assist community leaders in stimulating the innovation economy, building a local asset inventory and community brand, and leading the revitalization of their downtown cores.

Part Two, Building Social Capital through Collaboration and Inclusiveness introduces the concept of social capital and its importance in community revitalization efforts. The chapter on building collaboration offers a step-by-step approach for effective community decision making and strategies for conflict resolution. Ensuring that all community members are encouraged to play an active role in CED efforts requires focused approaches. Two of the many component sectors that require attentive strategies, namely youth and new Canadians, are examined and successful community approaches are highlighted. Practitioners are offered a variety of perspectives and resources.

The chapters comprising Part Three focus on new opportunities and approaches that provide economic renewal in rural communities. Insight into the emerging "creative rural economy" highlights the roles that CED practitioners and community leaders can play to support entrepreneurs and those engaged in the creative economy. As well, the document offers examples of how to grow the awareness and understanding of new economic opportunities that arise from adding value to current processes and products. Building on the value-added concept, the text describes the growing field of agritourism and offers several approaches for developing the tourism aspect of a local rural economy. Financing for entrepreneurial business ideas is often a major barrier to start-up and expansion plans. Part Three introduces several options for financing. Additional information and further resource details are provided in Part Four.

Part Four highlights some of the critical infrastructures required to support municipal and community efforts as they embrace new economic models. The definition of "community infrastructure" includes the social infrastructure that supports local economies. Medical and health services, built and natural recreational assets and the cultural infrastructure such as faith and arts amenities increasingly factor into the decisions about relocating a business or a family. Financing options including venture capital and angel investments are explored and recommendations are provided on how to facilitate access to funding.

While the text can be read iteratively, it is intended to serve as a practical reference manual. Where each chapter reflects the broader philosophy of CED detailed in Part One, it also stands alone and can be read in isolation to assist with specific challenges a practitioner or community leader may face. Theoretical arguments are not presented, so chapters can be read out of sequence. Some chapters are more detailed than others in order to serve an audience with varying CED experience. Readers should skim material that is already familiar and read more carefully material that is new. Throughout the chapters, a selection of real-life case studies document and show-case the strategies outlined in the text. They provide suggestions and point to possible courses of action but are not recipes for success. This is not an academic book but a practical guide. Throughout, we suggest additional reading and useful web links. Our goal is to provide the reader with a rich source of rural CED information.

Abbreviations

BIA	Business Improvement Association
CED	Community Economic Development
CFDC	Community Futures Development Corporation
CHFA	Canadian Health Foods Association
COIP	Canada-Ontario Infrastructure Program
DVA	Designated Viticultural Area
EDS	Entrepreneurial Development System
EIA	Economic Impact Analysis
EORN	Eastern Ontario Regional Network
ESL	English as a Second Language
ISP	Internet Service Provider
KIS	Knowledge Impact in Society
LEED	Leadership in Energy and Environmental Design
LETS	Local Exchange Trading Systems
OTMPC	Ontario Tourism Marketing Partnership Corporation
PEC	Prince Edward County
QSB	Queen's School of Business
RDÉE	Réseau de Développement Économique et d'Employabilité de l'Ontario
RDI	Rural Development Institute of Brandon University
RTO	Regional Tourism Organization
SCSES	South Central Settlement and Employment Services
SME	Small and medium-sized enterprise
SSHRC	Social Sciences and Humanities Research Council of Canada

PART ONE

Understanding Community Economic Development – New Roles for Practitioners

Rural and urban Canada are interdependent, particularly in metro-adjacent rural regions. Canada's balance of trade remains dependent on rural-based goods and much of its urban economy is linked to rural assets.[1] Traditionally, cities offered a concentration of specialized services, cultural and recreational venues, and educational and employment opportunities. In return, the countryside and adjacent rural towns and villages provided an important connection to the nation's heritage and to outdoor experiences linked to a wealth of natural assets.

The myriad challenges facing rural Eastern Ontario, discussed in the Preface, pose a challenge for traditional economic development approaches. In this text, we focus on community, not regional, development, but we refer to both, recognizing that the rural community functions as part of a region (e.g., Eastern Ontario), nation, and global economy. The community faces a range of internal and external constraints, some of which can be adjusted (e.g., broadband availability) and others that are difficult to change (e.g., location). Which factors are important, what are the CED priorities, and who bears the cost of community development varies widely.

To address changes and challenges in rural communities, it is important to examine the components of community revitalization and the evolving roles that practitioners of community economic development play to support revitalization efforts. This is our goal in Part One.

> "People need to have a common set of facts that they can debate. This in turn leads them to create a common understanding and language for the issues they are passionate about."
>
> David Pecaut – civic leader, city builder, strategist

1

Community Economic Development – Shifting the Focus to Local Self-reliance and an Innovation Economy

Community Economic Development (CED) involves a holistic planning approach. It shifts control of the local economy away from larger markets and remote decision makers towards local efforts. Economic development in communities is intimately connected with political, social, and environmental issues, and must consider all these. A structured approach to economic development is a priority for community stakeholders looking to grow their local economy in a sustainable fashion. Basic goals include increasing economic activity, improving employment prospects, and increasing the standard of living.

THE BEGINNINGS OF CED – FOUNDATION AND PRINCIPLES

Widespread support for CED in North America can be traced back to the economic recession of the early 1980s when basic assumptions about economic development began to be questioned. Previously, it was thought that the government would ensure high levels of employment, increased standards of living, appropriate services, and a reduction in regional disparities. In the US and Canada, dwindling state and provincial funds, combined with decision makers who were far removed and detached from local contexts, resulted in a wave of community degradation, both on a physical and social level. Community degradation often continues today, with pressures including globalization; wealth drain by large, externally owned corporations; environmental degradation and depleted natural resources; decreased citizen control as decisions are made by higher levels of government and large corporations; and the erosion of local culture and identity as communities feel pressured to conform to a homogeneous mass society.

CED goes beyond the older school of thought which equated economic development with growth. This more traditional approach, often referred to as "smokestack chasing," was based on the belief that almost all opportunities to attract investment should be taken, with the end goal being an increase in local economy size. From this perspective, a primary role of planners was to attract capital to the community by promoting the advantages to potential prospects (e.g., inexpensive land and labour, low taxes, lax environmental laws). However, this tended not to be connected with a larger more systematic strategy that considered the community as a whole, and consequently often led to unexpected and detrimental consequences, including:

- *Failure of existing businesses*. For example, large shopping centres could replace established local merchants.
- *Increased costs*. Higher rents and wages due to growth could make locally owned businesses less viable.
- *Environmental degradation*. Industrial and natural resource-based activities, such as mining, could pollute local water sources and disrupt flora and fauna, and ultimately hamper long-term development opportunities.

CED stems from the recognition that in order to curb community degradation and to stimulate sustainable economic development, a certain measure of community control is necessary. This idea affirms that communities cannot rely only on the government for effective planning. Bottom-up decision making is also needed. Likewise, communities cannot rely on large corporations and markets to ensure their survival. CED rejects the notion that a healthy economy at the national level will have trickle-down effects that ensure the economic health of communities at lower levels.

CONCEPTUALIZING CED

A useful way of conceptualizing and thinking about CED is in terms of community problem-solving. Ron Shaffer and his colleagues took this approach when developing their 'Star' model of CED.[1] Three of

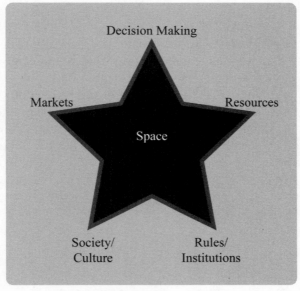

Figure A – The Community Economic Development "Star"

Source: Ron Shaffer, Steve Deller, & Dave Marcouiller, "Rethinking Economic Development," *Economic Development Quarterly* 20 no. 1 (February 2006): 59–74.

the nodes are specifically economics-related (markets, resources, and space), while the other three nodes are more broadly related to CED.

Space

Although some would argue space is no longer a key factor due to modern communication technologies, many rural Canadian communities lack broadband coverage and are, therefore, not surprisingly, still affected by space-based decisions. These decisions are made by businesses and households, for example. Businesses must decide where to locate, where to expand, where to acquire supplies, and where to market their products. Families must decide where to live, where to work, where to go to school and where to shop. Today, many of these decisions connect people with other communities beyond their residential locality. Communities need not view themselves as completely isolated but, rather, can actively organize, facilitate, and manage intercommunity connections.

Resources

Shaffer argues that in order to broaden the development policies available to communities, thinking must move beyond conventional perspectives of economic resources that are often limited to land, labour, capital and production technology. Traditionally, community policies of economic growth and development focused narrowly on attracting labour and capital, which seldom resulted in expected growth and at times had unexpected negative effects. Acknowledging and considering other more latent resources, such as the ability to innovate, is necessary to develop more effective policies. The ability to create new products, services, and production methods is essential for twenty-first century prosperity and survival.

Markets

Markets influence the demand for goods and services. Local markets consist of businesses and consumers within the community and the transactions between them. Non-local markets refers to community-produced goods and services that are sold outside of the community. The degree to which market transactions are more or less local affects the economic well-being of local residents.

Rules and Institutions

Traditionally, economic development planners primarily considered formal regulations and institutions, such as income tax laws, government power, and land and ownership rights. CED considers these, but also recognizes the power of informal rules and institutions including social organizations, culture, and community norms and values. These are less explicit than their formal counterparts, and differ in terms of enforcement, the latter being enforced largely via peer pressure and social sanctioning. Both formal and informal rules and institutions affect the functioning of communities in all spheres including economic, political, and social.

Society and Culture

It is important to consider the social structure and cultural norms and values that constitute a community's business climate. This includes attitudes towards inter- and intra-community communications, innovation, institutional capacity, and entrepreneurship. For example, do community attitudes support the necessary and often unsuccessful experimentation required to continuously innovate? Also, is failure and/or succeeding beyond the average frowned upon? Such attitudes can often be more powerful than formalized regulations and policies, and therefore must be considered.

Decisions

A community's ability to make effective decisions revolves around correctly identifying problems and then determining and implementing solutions. Implicit in effective decision-making is the ability to differentiate between causes and symptoms of problems. Addressing symptoms will not solve underlying problems. For instance, many rural communities have difficulty persuading businesses to locate in their area. A common response is to lower taxes as a means of attraction. Although this may indeed attract some businesses, often a bigger problem is that community members lack the skills and abilities that businesses require of employees. Therefore, a more effective solution than tax breaks may be to develop a program that facilitates the education and skills training of community members.

Another important part of decision-making is prioritization. All communities face more problems than they are able to address and, often, many challenges are beyond the community's control. Establishing a clear and generally agreed upon community vision which includes explicit values should guide the prioritization of issues as they arise.

Another challenging aspect of decision-making is determining an appropriate action plan. Once a strategy has been developed to address a problem or set of problems, community stakeholders must come together to agree on, and implement, a plan, otherwise few gains will be made. Communities differ in terms of their propensity for action-taking. This is largely determined by community culture, which should be considered. A culture that lacks an action-orientation can be an impediment. Finally, it is critical to recognize that decision-making is a continuous process that requires re-visitation and analyses of community values, priorities, and problems.

ECONOMIC SELF-RELIANCE — THE FUNDAMENTAL PRINCIPLE OF CED

The principles of CED are based on an integration of economic and noneconomic factors in the development of a long-term strategy. This strategy should reflect a comprehensive understanding of the range of choices available. This is not to say that short-term tactics and projects should not be considered, but rather, the long-term strategy can be viewed as being partly made up of short-term projects that are coordinated in an integrative and strategic fashion. Here, in comparison to simple economic growth notions, development is seen as an enhanced capacity to act and innovate, usually involving structural changes such as new ownership patterns; industry, product, or occupational mixes; technologies; and/or institutions. This requires that communities develop a certain level of economic self-reliance.

Gaining economic self-reliance is somewhat antithetical to global economic perspectives that focus on imports/exports and mass production and consumption. Self-reliance is based on orienting planning strategies towards local markets. This consists of producing internally and consuming much of that production internally so that wealth can be retained by the community, rather than flowing out into the larger, global market. This is not an isolationist approach. CED recognizes that flows of products and capital need to be exchanged with parties outside of the community; however, these flows need to be managed in a way that does not lead to community dependency or exploitation. The goal is to create trade alliances and partnerships that are based on reciprocal exchanges that equally benefit both sides. For instance, developing nations often do not fare well when they trade their primary resources for finished products from developed nations because the process of finishing products creates new businesses and, hence, wealth.

There are a number of ways for communities to generate and retain wealth. Imports can be a source of economic leakage. When goods or services produced outside the community are purchased, money flows from the community to external suppliers. Creating a community culture that encourages purchasing from local businesses, rather than buying from national or transnational chain stores can help limit external money flows. The key to successful import replacement is setting up local markets for local products

---

Wealth Creation through Innovation – the Tall Grass Prairie Bread Co.
A good example of wealth creation through innovation is the Tall Grass Prairie Bread Co. workers' co-operative in Winnipeg (http://www.tallgrassbakery.ca). Many years ago they decided to operate their own small flour mill, which allowed them to purchase wheat from local farmers. This innovation bypassed large transnational milling companies and enabled the bakery to cut production costs to the point where they could purchase local wheat for double what it sells on the market and still make a profit. Today, the bakery has created new employment opportunities for local residents, is supporting local farmers, and is providing healthy bread to local consumers. It illustrates the importance and potential of community innovation.

---

where buyers and sellers can make pre-arranged trade agreements. Before this can be done, information needs to be collected on what imported goods are being purchased in large quantities, and the existence of local suppliers who can provide similar products.

Another potential source of money leakage comes from bank savings. When people put their money into bank savings, the local community can lose because banks tend to reinvest money outside the region. To address this problem, community credit unions such as VanCity in Vancouver have set up community investment accounts to loan money to local businesses. Another solution that has been implemented in rural towns in Saskatchewan and Manitoba is the issuing of "local currency" by credit unions. Such programs lend out cash which can only be used at local businesses and provide a three-month, interest-free period of repayment. Finally, some communities in British Columbia have created local exchange trading systems (LETS) which track debits and credits of trading. These systems manage the trading of products and services without reliance on actual cash. This allows for multilateral exchanges even when cash is in low supply. The result is increased community purchasing power and new wealth.

Finally, one of the most important ways to create new wealth within communities is through innovation. Inventing new ways to create products from existing resources allows communities to generate wealth that did not previously exist and also allows for import substitution.

INNOVATION – A NECESSARY CED COMPONENT

The importance of innovation planning has increased in today's knowledge economy. In contrast to product and production efficiency that were the primary drivers of the industrial economy, today's economy relies on information and how it is used in the production of new ideas. Many small rural communities have found it difficult to adapt. Their strategies and planning still tend to reflect old practices developed to improve functioning in the industrial economy. However, increasing pressures from globalization and technological advancements are bringing change, including a greater awareness of the underlying dynamics of today's innovation economy and related functional practices that ensure survival and competitiveness.

The Innovation Economy – What Is It? How Does It Function?

The notion that innovation is the key driver of the economy stretches back to the pioneering work of Marx and Schumpeter who suggested that innovation is the main source of competitive advantage in capitalist economies.[2] Innovation is defined as "the process of bringing any new problem-solving idea into use ... it is the generation, acceptance, and implementation of new ideas, processes, products, or services."[3]

This definition can be broken down into two main parts: (1) The development of a creative idea, that is, an idea that is new and useful; (2) The implementation of the idea in some meaningful way. Obviously, the second depends on the first, and therefore as a first step, we must understand how creative ideas are born. What researchers have discovered is that creative ideas operate according to Darwinian evolutionary principles. Put differently, creativity is somewhat dictated by chance and serendipity; there is no guarantee that efforts will translate into a new and useful idea. It is only when the right information and ideas are combined in the right way at the right time that creativity comes to fruition. However, creative pursuits are by definition ambiguous because one does not know

> "Creative and innovative communities must support a culture and social fabric that encourages the questioning of current thinking and ways of doing things."
>
> Jeff Dixon

exactly what, and when, information is required, nor does one ever have unlimited access to unlimited information.

Still, humans have an extraordinary ability to be creative, and the odds of success are improved when one has access to large quantities of disparate or seemingly unrelated bits of information that can be processed and combined in novel ways. So the question becomes, what are the conditions under which information flows and processing are optimal in communities?

The Impact of Social Institutions and Networks on Innovation

To answer this question, researchers have explored two key structural aspects of the environment that impact innovation: the institutional environment and networks.

THE INSTITUTIONAL ENVIRONMENT

Morgan suggests that institutions can play a key role in stifling innovation. In his words, "capitalism is an evolutionary process driven by technical and organizational innovation ... a process in which social institutions other than the market play a major role."[4] In other words, as recent research has shown, the innovation process is socially embedded and socio-cultural influences are just as important as economic considerations in determining the diffusion of ideas.[5]

Accordingly, social institutions play a pivotal role because they influence information exchange and processing through their shaping of social patterns. Jepperson characterizes these social patterns as socially constructed regulatory controls (e.g., rewards and sanctions) that ensure the continuation of the organizations.[6] These social patterns include conventions, rules, norms and routines that have at their core a shared acceptance and understanding. Institutions serve the purpose of making the collective social environment predictable for its actors; as Field puts it, institutions create "reciprocal expectations of predictability."[7] Thus, institutions create shared ground rules for social interactions.

While these ground rules create a safety net, they also engender patterned thinking which can stifle innovation. This patterned thinking is a subconscious lens through which individuals in the institution view the world, and accordingly shapes how information is processed. Institutions, therefore, often serve to suppress innovation which requires not just allowing the questioning of convention, but rewarding questioning.

As stated previously, in order for a novel idea to become an innovation it must be implemented in some way and then passed on to and accepted by others. Unfortunately, most truly novel ideas are often initially rejected by others because they run counter to established conventions. Essentially, conventions and established institutional ways of thinking blind individuals to the utility of novel ideas. Hargadon and Douglas acknowledge the paradoxical nature of this situation, noting, "without invoking existing understandings, innovations may never be understood and adopted in the first place. Yet by hewing closely to existing institutions, innovators risk losing the valued details, representing the innovation's true novelty."[8]

The role of innovators and their support structures (e.g., economic development practitioners), then, is not simply to create new ideas. They must also invest in gaining widespread acceptance of their ideas by marketing them in ways that can fit within the mindsets of potential adopters, while still demonstrating creative feasibility. The social nature of the innovation process has caused many superior ideas to be defeated by lesser ones. For instance, vhs won over Beta, and compact discs over mini discs. It is not just the objective value or utility of a creative idea that determines whether it becomes an innovation, but also the actions and strategies used to diffuse it.

NETWORKS AND CLUSTERS

Findings from the innovation literature suggest that clusters and networks of relationships also shape the information flows needed in the production and implementation of creative ideas. Indeed, depending on the structure of social systems, the diffusion of innovations can either be enhanced or obstructed. Social networks are a series of influence relationships that can help develop innovations through information exchange. The interactions within a social network allow innovations to spread and, as they do so, individuals form their own opinions about these new developments.[9]

Related to institutional structures, social networks are the institutional foundations of preference formation and decision making.[10] This is significant for innovation development and diffusion because innovations, by nature, disrupt social norms and structures, including institutional structures. When individuals in a social network are developing and adopting new norms, other individuals in the network are more willing to do the same.[11] Thus, social networks can be used to foster innovation. A related concept is social density which refers to the number of individuals in a particular network. As density increases, so does the diversity of information being exchanged, which can be used to encourage further innovation. As well, beyond the structural features of the network, trust is a key variable necessary for social networks to function effectively; trust is "the lubricant that makes the running of any group or organization more efficient."[12]

The Role of Community Development Practitioners

The above description of the drivers of innovation is based on the "assumption that innovation is an interactive and territorially-embedded process, stimulated and influenced by many actors and information sources located both in and outside of firms."[13] Networks and clusters are considered the means through which knowledge is synthesized and exchanged as innovation occurs. This recognizes that it is not single firms that innovate in isolation, but rather innovation is the product of the collective resources, knowledge, capabilities and other inputs of the members of networks and clusters.[14] In this context, community actors serve to provide normative structures that support stable interactions and communication amongst actors in the network.[15] Within this framework, the role of community development practitioners is to foster clustered and networked industries, information flows, and connectedness. Although some believe that peripheral communities do not have the means to be innovative,[16] recent research by Doloreux suggests that SMEs in five peripheral regions of Canada are engaged in innovative activities at levels similar to their metropolitan counterparts. Indeed, peripheral regions have the potential and capacity to significantly contribute to the innovation economy.

The Community Development Practitioner as
Innovation Broker

As such, community development practitioners must take on the role of innovation brokers who facilitate cross-network connections. This can be understood in the following way:

> Under the global innovation networks model, inventors serve as the intellectual powerhouses that conduct basic science research and/or design products and services that result in patentable inventions. Transformers provide multifunctional production and marketing services that convert inputs from inventors or other transformers into valuable business innovations for either internal or external customers. Financiers provide funding for both inventors and transformers, usually in return for intellectual property rights. Brokers serve as the matchmakers or facilitators in this system who find and connect the other three network entities. The global innovation networks model is a collaborative ecosystem that allows businesses to innovate faster and grow more quickly.[17]

A recent report by Collaborative Economics presents a model of innovation brokering that includes a series of six steps.[18]

1 Raise the Stakes: Introduce Innovation as the Imperative
2 Reassess the Region: Identify Current and Potential Sources of Innovation
3 Connect the Innovators: Conduct a Disciplined, Collaborative Process
4 Broker Breakthroughs: Help Innovators Take Collaborative Action
5 Network the Brokers: Accelerate and Expand Innovative Collaborations
6 Redefine Success: Change the Metrics in Economic Development

RAISING THE STAKES
This involves reorienting perspectives on development so that innovation becomes the imperative. Many Canadian communities continue to hold tight to the tried and trusted strategy of focusing on disconnected growth initiatives or "smokestack chasing." Such a

strategy is based on the belief that attracting investment to increase the size of the local economy is the most effective way to promote development. Today, these beliefs can be challenged and replaced with an understanding that innovation is currently driving the economy and hence development. To accomplish this, brokers can personally share the latest thinking on innovation with as many different types of actors in as many different types of networks as possible (e.g., business, government, and community). This can be done by getting innovation and innovation-related topics on the agenda of meetings of business, government, and community organizations and forums.

As well, a database of innovator contacts can be developed and maintained to facilitate the collection and distribution of innovation information, opportunities, and materials.

REASSESSING THE REGION
Reassessing a region or a smaller community involves the identification of innovation strengths and weaknesses, including potential sources of innovation. Reassessment typically focuses on the main cornerstones of innovation: assets, networks, culture, and community. Assets include R&D and technology from universities and colleges, talented people, financial capital, industry clusters, research institutes, major institutions, and physical infrastructure. Networks are the complex web of relationships among people and organizations that transfer information and knowledge and create new products, services, policies, and initiatives.

DiMaggio describes culture as functioning through the "interaction of shared cognitive structures and supra-individual cultural phenomena (material culture, media messages, or conversation, for example).[19] Culture influences cognitive structures that are used to interpret the information we receive from our environments. Innovation cultures support the development of creativity and risk taking, are accepting of new ideas and unconventional thinking, and are not failure averse.

The report lists key questions that can guide regional or community reassessments such as:

a What are our driving clusters and how innovative are they?
b How are innovation and entrepreneurship contributing to community vitality and quality of life?

c What are the strengths and weaknesses of the assets for community innovation? What is missing?
d How does the community mindset or culture support or inhibit innovation and entrepreneurship?
e What networks connect assets that support community innovation? How strong are they? What connections are missing?
f Is innovative and entrepreneurial talent attracted and retained?
g How does the community compare to benchmark regions with regard to the cornerstones of innovation?

CONNECTING THE INNOVATORS

The contacts and networks identified in the previous steps can be used to engage the drivers of innovation. This means systematically designing a cluster or process to convene innovators, such as an "opportunity mobilization" cluster or process. *The Industry Clusters of Opportunity User Guide* is a training resource prepared by Collaborative Economics, Inc. as a part of the California Regional Economies Project. The guide is designed with two important audiences in mind: workforce and economic development professionals. The guide assists professionals in developing an economic data set that can be used to drive decision making across many different areas including strategic planning, investment decisions, and policy changes. The guide also explains how to put a cluster of opportunity dataset to work, using the data to mobilize cluster employers as full partners in workforce and economic development. The guide can be found at http://labor.ca.gov/panel/pdf/Final_User_Guide_090607.pdf.

BROKERING BREAKTHROUGHS

In this step, innovators are helped to move from ideas to collaborative action. This involves the development of an action plan that explicates goals, outcomes, strategies and implementation requirements. In developing an action plan, *Collaborative Economics* recommends the consideration of the following elements:[20]

a Results – the specific, measurable "breakthrough" outcomes expected. What constitutes a breakthrough will depend on the scope, setting, and stage of community problem-solving.
b Roles – the specific roles implementation partners will play, depending on their unique capabilities.

c Relationships – the specific connections needed among partners, depending on the level of interdependence required to achieve the desired results.

d Agreements – specific actions that can be taken, often focused projects or initiatives, or mobilizations such as campaigns, and specific multi-party arrangements that establish specific commitments or guidelines for policy and action by partners.

e Accountability – specific and ongoing commitments to hold partners accountable for results, both through follow-on agreements and assessments of community competitiveness.

f Architecture – an organizational platform or web that provides the capacity to support, expand, and renew fledgling efforts, such as multi-party forums or networks.

NETWORKING THE BROKERS

Innovation is a continuous process of invention. Therefore the process of collaboration must also be continuous and not just a one-time event. To support the continuation of interactions among innovators, connections need to be formed among brokers. Not only will this help sustain collaboration, but it will increase the networking productivity by regularly stimulating new connections and opportunities for innovation. Therefore a connecting mechanism, such as a community forum, needs to be put in place.

REDEFINING SUCCESS

In order to sustain the innovation process, community development practitioners must redefine success incentives and metrics. Traditional metrics of economic success – quantity of jobs and number of firms attracted/retained – can be replaced or supplemented by those that accurately measure success in an innovation economy including quality of jobs, wage and income growth, and innovation (e.g., patents, commercialization, and start-ups).

SUMMARY

What is effective are "people and place" policies. What does not diffuse away quickly are infrastructure and workforce. Although a few key people may be mobile, large numbers of the workforce are not mobile. Policies that support the education and training of the workforce, that support research combined with education, that support a modern infrastructure, and support the development of institutions that facilitate collaboration between business, government, and the independent sector will have lasting effects of building capacity that does not diffuse away. Develop the people and places – the habitat for living and working.[21]

The current economy is markedly different from the industrial economy of days gone by. The shift towards an imperative of innovation requires a reorientation of both perspective and action. Thinking needs to reflect today's economic forces, and planned community action must harness these forces so that they are aligned. Key new roles for CED practitioners include serving as innovation brokers and network facilitators for entrepreneurs, businesses, and communities. As well, practitioners must redefine success in the innovation economy by focusing on the quality of work created as marked by income and wage growth, and innovation indicators such as patents and commercialization.

2

Community Assets – Essential Building Blocks for CED

The CED approach to revitalization efforts discussed in Chapter 1 depends on community leaders understanding and prioritizing available resources. Leaders benefit from having a comprehensive and up-to-date inventory of community assets. These assets include capacities of individuals, institutions and organizations, and physical resources.[1] The process of generating an asset inventory has several commonly-used names including asset mapping, mapping community capacity, and identifying community assets.

The creation of an asset inventory is of great value for a number of reasons. First, it presents community leaders with a broad and inclusive array of resources; this allows leaders to choose community development strategies that are in accordance with their asset base. Secondly, an asset inventory illuminates the gaps, needs, and inefficiencies in the region and helps community leaders to reallocate resources to key challenge areas and avoid unnecessary expenditures. Ultimately, an understanding of local resources helps shape the image with which a community presents itself to the world, playing a key role in community branding. As such, the creation of an inventory of community assets is undoubtedly a worthwhile goal.

CREATING AN ASSET INVENTORY

Asset identification consists of recognizing, categorizing, and cataloging all major assets that are relevant to economic development. Also recorded is information pertaining to these assets. For example, a college that exists in the community is considered an asset; in addition, to recording the name of the school, the names of the key

---

Some Canadian Communities with Asset Inventories
Penticton, British Columbia
http://www.footprintstotechnology.com/docs/INVENTORY-OF-ASSETS2010.pdf

Kapuskasing, Ontario (News Release regarding a new Asset Mapping Project, March 2009)
http://www.kapuskasing.ca/Documents/Businesses/Kapuskasing%20Final%20Strategy%20%20(Website).pdf

Southslave Region, North-West Territories
http://www.sshcp.nt.ca

---

administrators and contact information would also be documented. Eventually, this process will create a database that lists the assets and asset-related information to improve the decision-making of community leaders, and ultimately, the quality of community life.[2] Today, for an asset inventory to be most useful, it should be made available online to community members.

Step 1: Assigning a Leader and Assembling the Project Team

Creating an asset inventory is no small undertaking and requires both human and financial resources. Community leaders typically first appoint an individual in the community who will spearhead and manage the project. This leader would not only be responsible for creating an *initial* asset inventory, but he or she would also ensure that the asset inventory is updated on a frequent basis. In small rural communities, it may only be feasible to hire a single individual to undertake the entire initiative. However, in communities where there are more financial resources, there could be a project team.

Ideally, the project team would include people from the private, academic, public, and non-profit sectors, as well as individuals with knowledge of the workforce and the educational and economic development institutions in the region.[3] In resource-constrained situations, some of these individuals might volunteer time to help with identifying community assets. The team would also include an individual with strong research and analytical skills. Last, the team would include someone who is proficient at creating and managing a database where the community information would be stored and updated.

Step 2: Categorizing Community Assets – What Gets Recorded?

Broadly speaking, a community asset can be defined as *anyone or anything that can be used to improve the quality of community life.*[4] More specifically, assets include the human, intellectual, financial, physical, and institutional capital in a community. Traditionally, the asset base has included information for corporate location decisions such as the availability of skilled labour, the quality of transportation infrastructure, the cost of doing business, and proximity to customers. However today, even more critical assets are thought to be other factors important to innovation such as research and development investment, technology transfer, and entrepreneurship support programs.[5]

The major types of assets (with examples) that can be recorded are as follows:

- Individual capacities (e.g., information about community leaders)
- Human capital (e.g., primary, secondary, and post-secondary educational institutions)
- Research and development institutions (e.g., research centres and business incubators)
- Financial capital (e.g., venture capital firms)
- Industrial base (e.g., major employers)
- Connective organizations (e.g., business and economic development organizations)
- Legal and regulatory environment (e.g., local government)
- Physical infrastructure (e.g., natural resources)
- Quality of life (e.g., recreational facilities)

Under each "type" of asset, important information needs to be recorded. For instance, under "Industrial base," the following information about major employers could be recorded:

- List of largest employers in the region
- Names, location, and contact information for officers
- Applicable industrial codes
- Number of employees
- Product and service offerings

See Appendix A for a model template that could be adapted for use by the asset-inventory project team.

Step 3: Gathering Information about Assets

➢ *Information from Team Members*

As a starting point, it is best to record information about assets that members of the team already are familiar with. If team members come from a wide variety of functional backgrounds, they will be able to provide a great deal of information about the resources in the community. This will serve as a base level of information for the database.

➢ *Community Assets*

The majority of the information that is needed to create an asset inventory can often be found online. Today, the use of the Internet is often the primary method that members of the project team use to gather information. Search engines like Google and online databases are powerful tools. The yellow pages online (http://www.yellowpages.ca) can quickly provide a listing of businesses according to business type. Databases such as Proquest (http://www.proquest.com/en-US) contain news articles, journal publications, and government reports that can provide important demographic and statistical information. Additional databases can be used if team members can get access to university library resources (e.g., http://www.library.queensu.ca/research/databases). The Internet also contains the names and contact information of individuals who may be able to provide additional information about community assets.

➢ *Solicit Information*

Project team members should correspond with individuals who may have community asset information either by email or telephone. Team members should develop a protocol for soliciting information. This way, communications can be professional, which will make it more likely for information to be shared.

In order to get detailed information from community leaders about themselves, it is necessary to go beyond making phone calls and sending emails. To record individual details, researchers have come up with a variety of survey instruments (e.g., individual capacity inventories).[6] While these instruments vary considerably, they essentially all ask respondents to provide their names, contact

---

Discovery Workshop Background

From 2008–2010, the Monieson Centre at Queen's School of Business hosted a series of Discovery Workshops across Southern Ontario. These community workshops brought together academics with local business people, economic developers, and community leaders to identify the region's economic development priorities.

A key component of the workshops was developing an inventory of local economic development resources and knowledge. Over the course of twenty-four community workshops, the Monieson Centre developed a local knowledge asset inventory, identifying resources for pressing issues including, for example, youth retention, entrepreneurship, and the rural creative economy. Several communities used the identified priorities and assets to further develop action items for ongoing community development.

Workshop reports, which include local knowledge inventories, are available free on the Centre's rural economic revitalization website at http://www.easternontarioknowledge.ca.

---

information, skills and abilities, interests, entrepreneurial activities, and their affiliations with various community groups.

To create a survey, project team members can use an online survey creation tool such as Survey Monkey (http://www.surveymonkey.com). This tool should allow team members to create professional surveys at a low cost. Community leaders can then be invited to fill out surveys online. When the data is collected, the survey tool should present the data in a user-friendly format so that the information can be easily transferred to a database. In the end, this process should create a consolidated list or directory of a sample of community leaders that contains important information about their skills, abilities, interests, and backgrounds. Usually it is not possible to gather data from every community leader. The surveys should target leaders in each of the key sectors of the community (e.g., business, skilled trades, academia, non-profit, healthcare, and government). The goal would be to obtain data from a representative sample of community leaders.

Step 4: Building the Inventory and Keeping it Up-to-date

Ideally, the asset inventory should be online, accessible to members of the community to support informed decision making. The inventory needs to be kept up-to-date. Although resources will dictate the feasibility of updates, ideally revisions should occur at least once a year. This requires the team to collaborate periodically and repeat the information gathering process. For instance, new businesses, organizations, and institutions that have located in the area need to be recorded. By maintaining the asset inventory, community members will have a valuable resource for many years.

FROM INVENTORY TO IMAGE – BRANDING AND MARKETING IN RURAL COMMUNITY DEVELOPMENT

The inventory is a starting place for defining a community's unique identity. This unique identity combined with the "sense of place" is a key lever in attracting people and investment. Accordingly, place branding has emerged as a critical local economic development tool, allowing communities to promote their distinct identity through a unique brand. Identifying the most authentic, meaningful culture and identity assets in any given locale can prove challenging.

In reviewing an asset inventory, specific themes will begin to emerge that define the image or positioning for the community. There may be an abundance of natural attributes or heritage buildings or other special features that a community may want to highlight to attract visitors, new residents, or investors. These will influence the community brand and marketing strategy.

While logos and slogans are symbols of a brand, the total brand represents much more. A brand is a story, a means of standing out and demonstrating something unique about a community which sets it apart from others. Individuals in the community all have a role in the story, each with something unique to contribute towards the whole of the brand image. In addition, developing a brand may have unforeseen benefits like bringing the community closer together, providing a common, shared experience.

There are two key dimensions to brand knowledge:

· Brand Awareness: the ease with which a brand comes to mind when triggered by a specific need and the ability to recognize a particular brand

• Brand Image: the meaning(s) associated with the brand

For example, Niagara-on-the-Lake is associated with wine tours. It may also connote the Shaw Festival, a "quaint" downtown, or a popular location for weddings. Prince Edward County (e.g., Picton and the surrounding area) is emerging as a wine region competitor to Niagara-on-the-Lake; however, it serves a different populace (Eastern Ontario) seeking a similar experience.

CONSIDERATIONS WHEN DEVELOPING A BRAND

➢ *What kind of image should be portrayed?*
This will depend on the ultimate goals. Possible objectives might be:

• Tourism: If the goal is to develop the area as a getaway, specific services and infrastructure (e.g., restaurants, lodging, and entertainment) may be needed. In this case, the government may be a good source of information and potential partnerships.[7] A possible avenue to explore for generating tourism might be the hosting of an annual event, such as the Havelock Country Jamboree.[8] Another potential approach might be promoting the community as a location to purchase or rent a vacation home.
• Economic Growth: If the community seeks to develop a brand for attracting industries, what elements (e.g., services, skilled labour, and infrastructure) make the community attractive? A consideration for this goal is that the community may become dependent on a single industry and suffer greatly should that employer leave, as has happened in many manufacturing-based communities, e.g., the Hershey factory closing in Smiths Falls, Ontario.[9] On the other hand, a review of existing trades may provide opportunities to exploit or expand these resources. For example, Wellington North Township (an area north of Guelph, Ontario) recognized an abundance of local bakeries and began marketing the area as the Butter Tart Trail.[10]
• Increasing Permanent Residents: Some communities have sought to take advantage of the projected increase in retirees as a result of aging baby boomers by creating Adult Lifestyle Communities, as exemplified by the Wilmot Creek development east of Toronto.[11] Elliot Lake, located about halfway between North Bay and Sault Ste. Marie, has successfully marketed the community as a destination for retirees. As a result, vacancy rates have

Branding and Marketing Experiences in Hastings County
"I have been directly involved in three key branding initiatives aimed at attracting more investment to the local area, and in two cases, had an additional goal of attracting more tourists. Our first broad-based branding initiative was *Comfort Country*, representing the rural communities of Madoc, Marmora, Stirling & Tweed. First coined in 2003, the slogan was reviewed and enhanced in 2006 through a local Main Street Revitalization Initiative. Following an extensive data collection and consultation exercise, the brand changed to *Destination Comfort Country: Madoc, Marmora, Stirling & Tweed, Explore the Four*. A strategic plan of implementation and roll-out was prepared including published lure materials, publications, posters for all store windows, re-useable shopping bags and a new website at http://www.comfortcountry.ca. A well-attended public launch was held to get the word out about the brand and promote its use.

"The second initiative is Hastings County's new investment marketing brand *Communities with Opportunities*. With the support of an experienced marketing consultant, the county embarked on a formal visioning and branding exercise to highlight our assets and strengths and to develop an investment marketing brand to attract our target investment audience. We identified that we were *Communities with Opportunities* offering a place for anyone to live, retire, invest, run a business, and feel welcome no matter who they were or what they wanted to do. We have since integrated this brand into our online blog http://www.communitieswithopportunities.ca and on our Twitter, YouTube, and other social media sites.

"It is important to remember that branding is more than just a logo or tagline. It is essentially figuring out what your community has to offer, what makes it different from the rest, and then figuring out who might want to buy or experience that. The final step is packaging – taking what makes your community unique and getting the message across to the identified target audience. Maybe your community has some unique agricultural product that nobody else has. Or maybe some crazy historical event happened in your town that might be of interest to a certain crowd. Building your message around those attributes will help your community stand out from the rest.

"Simply saying that your community is a 'Four Season Playground' or 'The Gateway' to something else just will not work."

Andrew Redden, economic development manager,
Hastings County

dropped and the community has seen an increase in new services and amenities.[12]

This type of planning has both pitfalls and benefits. For instance, an aging population may need infrastructure and services that are not available in a small community (e.g., hospitals). This can be viewed as a migration limitation but can also provide opportunities for the development of local industries, resulting in new jobs for the community.

➤ *What is the community support for this image or brand?*
Perhaps one of the most important elements in developing a community brand is to ensure that as many people from the community as possible support the chosen image. While in a business situation the brand image can come from the business owner or the CEO, a community is more democratic and individual members can choose to ignore an image if it does not suit them. As a result, it is important to get people involved early in the branding process. Leaders must elicit feedback from residents about what makes the community special and distinct.

➤ *Partnerships vs. differentiation?*
In thinking about how to define a community, many group levels may come to mind. A church or social group is a community, just as a town or a township is a community. In trying to decide how to brand a community, a good starting place is defining the boundaries of what residents consider to be *their* community. In some cases, a group of individual towns will share a collective identity which can create a regional brand. Although coordinating across multiple towns may have some inherent difficulties with regards to making decisions and getting complete buy-in, there are many advantages to this approach. For example, the development and communication

costs can be shared among more people, reducing the costs borne by each individual. As well, if the goal is tourism, different attractions in various areas may be packaged together.

Once the boundaries have been determined, the competition can be identified and examined. While the community and its goals may be similar to others in different regions, these somewhat similar communities are not necessarily in direct competition if they serve different customer bases. Local offerings should also be compared with other communities' amenities. For example, is the community closer to its customer base than its competitors? Does the community have facilities that others lack? These differences begin to form the starting point for establishing a target market, and will help decide how to communicate the brand message.

➢   *Who is the target market?*

The target market will depend on the overall goal behind creating the community brand. For example, it will differ if the community is seeking to increase tourism versus permanent residence. Determining the characteristics of the target market early on in the brand development process will help ensure brand communications appeal to target audiences. It can reduce the required marketing resources and lead to a very direct communications approach. This clear focus should be balanced; a narrow message may not appeal to many people.

Traditionally, people have categorized target markets by (1) Demographic factors (e.g., age, income, and geographical location), and (2) Interests (e.g., active or passive lifestyle, recreational interests, and social memberships).

To continue with our example, the target market's age group may be a factor in both increasing tourism (e.g., the services and attractions may appeal to a limited age group) and attracting permanent residents (e.g., establishing the community as a retirement locale). The geographic location of the target market is an important consideration from a competition perspective (i.e., who else is trying to reach this group?) and also from a brand message perspective (i.e., is the community promoted as a place to visit in a single day, or as a place to stay for an extended period?).

➢   *Can the strengths of the community match the interests of the target?*

Hiking trails and outdoor activities are better suited to individuals who are looking for an active lifestyle or vacation destination, while cultural attractions like museums may be more appealing to a different market segment. Current cultural trends may also be considered when defining a target market. For example, Haliburton has taken advantage of their natural resources by offering an attraction geared towards people seeking an eco-friendly destination.[13] This type of attraction allows them to seek out target segments which include tourists with an interest in the environment, school field trips, and people looking for an adventurous outing.

> *How can the message get out?*

Once a clear brand identity has been established, the focus shifts to communicating this image to others. While a large budget might allow for broad-sweeping forms of communication like television advertisements and radio spots, many communities will need to use a more targeted approach. At this point, knowing the target market becomes vital. Brainstorming ways to reach the target market can breed creative ideas that provide new ways of differentiating the community. Also, a review of available resources – both public (e.g., federal and provincial government programs) and private (e.g., local companies that have resources for generating communications) – can help make an effective communications plan.

A website is often a good place to start. However, this is a starting point, not an end in itself. In developing a communications plan, passive communications should be balanced with active ones. For example, a website is generally regarded as a passive medium; that is, it relies on the customer seeking out the community. Being proactive is much more difficult, but can also be more effective. For example, if the goal is to attract new industries, local leaders can start looking into organizations involved in these industries. Organizational websites and news sources can give an indication as to which companies are growing or shrinking, and which ones might have a need which the community can serve. Volunteers can be recruited to contact these organizations and establish a relationship with them, to sell the community as a possible location for future growth.

> *How will success be measured?*

Brands require maintenance and adjustments. A marketing plan should include techniques for monitoring and evaluating the success of the community branding, as well as options for expanding the communications reach.

Specifically, milestones and criteria for evaluating the success of the plan should be set from the outset. These points for evaluation should be realistic, but also reflect achievements that are directly related to the branding efforts. For example, if the objective is to increase tourism, the number of *new* visitors to the area (as opposed to those who have visited previously), or repeat visitors over a period of time, can be tracked and compared with past experiences.

Whether the objectives relate to tourism, permanent residents, new industries, or other creative initiatives, one of the best sources of information are the people themselves. Local leaders can find out why people and businesses came to the community, what they think of the community, and what makes the community unique or special. When local residents travel, they can ask the people in the area they visit about their home community to find out the level of awareness regarding the brand (e.g., "What do you think of when you think about *community x?*"). Not only will this provide information about the awareness of the community brand, but it will also give feedback on how the message is being interpreted. In all cases of branding, the vital part is not necessarily the image conveyed, but how people actually interpret and respond to the image, and ultimately how successful the branding is in achieving the desired objectives.

SUMMARY

Getting the word out about the community's identity and unique attributes and offerings is an important aspect of revitalizing a community. Place branding has emerged as a critical local economic development tool, allowing communities to promote their distinct identity through a unique brand. Communities often expend considerable resources creating promotional materials and campaigns to attract businesses, visitors, and new residents. CED professionals can be instrumental in helping a community to develop a greater understanding and appreciation of an asset-based approach to marketing and branding. A key building block for revitalization is the creation of an asset inventory. CED practitioners can assist local leaders with the development of a comprehensive database and a process to ensure that the inventory is kept up to date. Together, with local leaders and the community, the practitioner can analyze the data and explore community strengths and gaps. Specific themes that emerge from the review help to define the image or positioning for the community. This, in turn, leads to a greater understanding of the community's unique identity or sense of place – a key lever for attracting people and investment. Communities are encouraged to examine their brand awareness and image and understand which target markets they currently attract or want to attract prior to embarking on branding and marketing campaigns.

3

The Importance of the Downtown Core

VIBRANT DOWNTOWNS AND MAIN STREETS

Downtowns play a crucial role in the economic health of a town or city. Downtowns that are vibrant stimulate economic and business activity in the community and attract visiting tourists. A sizable share of a town's or a city's tax base is derived from its downtown economic activity. In addition, downtowns embody the heritage of a community and portray the image that people have of the town or city. Currently, an aesthetically pleasing downtown that is full of activity, particularly pedestrian activity, conveys a positive and attractive image of the community, which in turn attracts more visitors to the downtown core. As such, creating a vibrant downtown should be an important goal for community leaders.

What strategies help to create a vibrant downtown?

➢ *Establish a leadership team with purpose and vision*

The first step in creating a vibrant downtown is for community leaders to become committed to taking action. Community leaders should organize themselves to work together in a team or a committee (e.g., a revitalization steering committee) to provide human and financial resources. Research demonstrates that such committees help stakeholders work together for mutual benefit.

Downtown revitalization is a complex process and requires effort on many different fronts. Therefore, it is best to bring together a diverse group, possessing a variety of interests, perspectives, and resources. Typical committee members represent:

- A business improvement association (BIA) (focus on promotion of retail sales)

- The Chamber of Commerce (fosters tourism and business recruitment)
- The municipal government (provides leadership to the municipality and works to maintain a strong tax base to provide adequate municipal services and infrastructure improvements)
- Building owners (interested in business growth and may be considering building renovation and renewal projects)

Once the team is brought together, meetings should be arranged to determine key issues, challenges, and opportunities facing the downtown area. Community leaders should establish an overall vision for revitalization efforts. This can unite stakeholders despite their diverse interests. Last, a detailed work plan should be created to turn the identified desired results into reality.[1] The vision and work plan form are critical foundations for fundraising and grant application efforts.

➤ *Promote diversity of use*

A classic urban design principle for downtown revitalization is to promote diversity of use.[2] Vibrant downtowns provide a varied and lively business and leisure environment. This brings different types of people downtown for different reasons at various times of the day, week and year. As such, community leaders should keep diversity in mind when making plans to use vacant buildings and land. For instance, a disproportionate amount of office space might make the downtown area dead in the evenings. In this case, community leaders could try to attract businesses that provide entertainment activities (e.g., restaurants, clubs, and movie theatres) to bring people downtown at night and on weekends.

A recent strategy to make downtowns multifunctional is to promote the creation of downtown housing.[3] This provides increased traffic and a human presence during non-business hours and increases the market for downtown businesses.[4] This also promotes the downtown's image as a safe area. Community leaders can encourage real estate developers to provide housing in the downtown core. This housing can be marketed to singles, young professionals, empty-nesters, and seniors.

➤ *Improve pedestrianization*

Pedestrianization, or walkability, focuses on making the downtown more pedestrian friendly. This is beneficial for a number of reasons. First, having more pedestrians increases downtown economic activity, as more goods and services are demanded. Secondly, pedestrians

8–80 Cities
http://www.8-80cities.org

8–80 Cities is a Canadian based non-profit organization with a mission to contribute to the creation of vibrant cities and healthy communities, where residents are happier and enjoy great public places.

The origin of the name stems from their signature line urging leaders to make decisions about their built environment based on what would be good for an 8-year-old and an 80-year-old which would result in great cities for all.

A number of Ontario communities including Caledonia and Halton Hills have completed Community Action Plans for Life that incorporate recommendations for increasing the "walkability" of their downtown areas.

improve the downtown's image. Researchers suggest that the positive image of a downtown is gauged more so by the volume of pedestrian activity than by economic indicators.[5] Without pedestrians, a downtown can look lifeless and uninteresting, no matter how aesthetically pleasing the area may be.

The quality of the experience of walking through a downtown is a key measure of its success. As such, despite the importance of vehicular access and parking, pedestrians should be given clear priority in certain areas to encourage walking. People will choose to walk in downtown spaces if they are comfortable, convenient, safe, interesting, beautiful, and enjoyable. This can be done by:[6]

- Widening and maintaining sidewalks and walkways
- Improving safety and security
- Reducing traffic speeds
- Ensuring overall cleanliness
- Promoting environmental friendliness (e.g., by providing recycling disposal bins)
- Creating more sitting spaces
- Making streets easier to cross by adding crosswalks
- Making streetscape improvements to beautify the downtown environment (e.g., by adding flowers, trees, interesting lighting, attractive pavement, banners, brick pavers)[7]

St. Thomas, ON – Canada's Railway Capital
http://www.narhf.org/
Every August, people from St. Thomas and visitors from far
and wide come to celebrate the railway influence in the Iron
Horse Festival. In addition to preserving an important historical landmark, the project also promises to rejuvenate the
downtown core and serve as a testament to the enduring legacy
the railways have left on St. Thomas, Canada's railway capital.
A fundraising campaign has been underway to restore the
Canada Southern Railway Station located in St. Thomas,
Ontario. Originally built in 1872, this unique and historic
facility is a designated heritage railway station under the Canadian Heritage Railway Stations Protection Act.

- Encouraging business owners to have attractive building facades,
  awnings, and store windows
- Locating parking facilities in less conspicuous places as parking
  facilities can be a major pedestrian impediment

One city that has been successful in beautifying its downtown
area to increase "pedestrianization" is Brandon, Manitoba. Community leaders planted trees, replaced old signs with newer brighter
signs, installed wrought iron benches, built heritage lamp posts,
and installed matching garbage containers, fencing, and antique fire
hydrants. These improvements have made Brandon's downtown a
pedestrian friendly area.[8]
Another important town planning principle is density. Jane Jacobs,
a well-known and respected writer on urban planning, emphasizes
the importance of density in the downtown, and acknowledges how
it promotes pedestrian traffic.[9] Density creates a critical mass of
activity easily accessible by foot. Even small gaps in the continuity
of buildings can inhibit the flow of pedestrian activity.[10]
➤ *Encourage historic preservation and building renovations*
Many rural downtowns have architecturally distinctive old buildings
that are attractive and represent a downtown's heritage. These buildings create a downtown's sense of community and sense of place.
Unfortunately, in many cases these structures are underused, empty,

---

Waynesville Antique and Merchant Advertising Association
http://www.waynesvilleshops.com

In Waynesville, Ohio, there are a number of stores that sell antique goods. These merchants have created a niche, coming together to form the Waynesville Antique and Merchant Advertising Association. With no paid staff, they manage to spend thousands of dollars a year on advertising.

---

or rundown. By preserving old, historic downtown buildings, communities can help to make their downtowns more appealing. This, in turn, attracts others, both residents and tourists. More attractive downtowns should also attract more private investment. In a survey of fifty-seven small cities in North America, historic preservation was cited as the most common downtown revitalization strategy.[11]

Preservation efforts can consist of renovating a storefront or building facade. It can also consist of converting and renovating buildings for different uses. For example, a structure built for one purpose (e.g., a railroad terminal, theatre) can be used quite differently (e.g., as a restaurant, commercial building). To encourage preservation activity, community leaders can provide downtown store owners with financial incentives for façade beautification. Community leaders can also encourage financial institutions to provide low-interest loans to businesses engaging in renovation efforts of historic structures.

It should be noted that preservation activities require careful planning. Renovated buildings should be integrated with the character and fabric of the downtown design. To ensure this is done, communities can establish design guidelines and regulations.[12] Some communities have designated a "Code Enforcement Officer" who grants permission for external changes made to buildings. A less strict approach is to use design guidelines that are voluntary unless tied to financial assistance. Design experts or assistance committees can help building owners to implement upgrades that are in accordance with design regulations.

➤ *Identify and promote niches*

Many downtowns have numerous businesses that offer similar products or services, and create a "niche" or "cluster." For example, in Picton, Ontario (http://www.picton-bia.on.ca), many artisans and artists have opened studios. Several stores sell local art and hand-crafted products. Picton can be thought of as having an "artisan niche" or "arts cluster." Community leaders can encourage businesses that offer the same products and services to work together. By joining forces, these businesses can pool their resources to create an advertising and promotional campaign that would be beyond what they could individually afford. A town or city's chamber of commerce can also engage in promoting a niche, e.g., to boost tourism. Together, these organizations can communicate to customers that the downtown area offers a broad selection of a particular merchandise or service. Several promotional strategies that have been used by various communities to promote niches include:

- Creating a specific website for the downtown area
- Ensuring that a niche is mentioned on other websites relating to the town or city
- Creating a billboard on a major highway
- Displaying advertisements in major newspapers or magazines
- Running radio or television advertisements

Eventually, a city or town's downtown area can become well-known and celebrated for its niche, attracting more individuals and businesses to the downtown core. Pulling it all together takes vision and dedication. The community of Terrace Bay, Ontario (http://www.terracebay.ca) demonstrates economic development in action and results, from leadership at various (e.g., municipal and community) levels to collaboration between the public and private sectors; and, from setting an aggressive course for revitalization to embarking on new construction.

SUMMARY

Healthy and vibrant downtowns boost economic health and quality of life in rural communities. Thriving downtown cores also stimulate new business and job creation thereby increasing the community's options for goods and services. A healthy downtown builds pride in its heritage. Successful downtown revitalization efforts encourage citizens to become involved in creating the community's future. They include a broad-based strategy for a multi-functional

**Terrace Bay – Entrepreneurial Community Award of the Year
2010–11**

It took a strong entrepreneurial spirit and vision of a brighter
future to see the people of Terrace Bay through one of the most
difficult economic downturns this small northern Ontario
town has ever experienced.

Located on the north shore of Lake Superior, east of Thunder
Bay, this small community of 1,700 people was built around
a pulp and paper mill in the 1940s that at its peak employed
more than 1,000. However, during the last two years, an ailing
forestry sector resulted in the layoff of the entire workforce of
420 people, leaving a startling 40 per cent unemployment rate.

In what appeared to be the end of the township's economic
lifeline, the paper mill sat idle under creditor protection, unable
to pay its taxes. However, council remained hopeful and rallied
for financial support from the provincial government for the
mill along with funding for other economic diversification projects to breathe some life back into the community.

"They [council] said, 'We can't just sit back and hope something happens. We have to look toward the future' ... They
were committed to it, and administration took it and ran with
it," said CAO Carmelo Notarbartolo.

With the council's support, advocacy, and perseverance, Terrace Bay Pulp Inc. was able to obtain a $25 million loan from
the Ontario government. Other money from a private financier
was coming, leaving the township hopeful that the mill would
return to full production of 1,200 tonnes of pulp per day.

Other diversification efforts were initiated about four years
ago when council completed a strategic plan, which it has
aggressively implemented. A $3 million downtown revitaliza-
tion project helped give a facelift to the core businesses with
new canopies, landscaping enhancements, and a fifty-foot
lighthouse with an observation deck, visible from the Trans-
Canada Highway and providing a view of Lake Superior, the
township, and the downtown.

"We're hoping the lighthouse will hook travellers into our
downtown core," Notarbartolo said, explaining that Ministry
of Transportation statistics indicate 800,000 vehicles pass by

Terrace Bay every year. "Even attracting a small percentage of them to spend some money in our downtown will generate new revenue for our downtown businesses." New highway signage and in-town signs have been erected to promote tourism attractions like the gorge, beach, and golf course.

The project prompted a local pharmacy to expand its services and staff as a direct result. A $2 million cultural centre was created through the renovation of an old elementary school. It now houses a new library, seniors activity centre, and community hall. With the community's aging population, the seniors centre has provided a space for recreational activities as well as a place to gather. The community hall has already booked events and weddings, generating some employment and keeping people in the community. Previously, events and weddings took place outside of Terrace Bay in nearby Schreiber. Partnerships with nearby townships like Schreiber, Jackfish, and Rossport have helped strengthen each other's position when applying for government funding.

In 2011, Notarbartolo said they expected to see the full impact of the projects. "It's been some very tough times but there is a light at the end of the tunnel," he said. "All the little things in the strategic plan have evolved successfully and now the mill will be back up and running. We're very excited about the next twelve months in Terrace Bay."

Author: Adelle Larmour, Northern Ontario Business Awards

A news story issued in March 2013 indicates that the anticipated growth is taking hold and more is expected. "The local pulp mill was sold to the Aditya Birla Group as part of a $250 million planned investment in the AV Terrace Bay Inc. operation. Also, the Community has seen the recent completion of the Terrace Bay Cultural Centre, the Wilkes Terrace Long Term Care Facility and the Terrace Bay Downtown Revitalization Project."[*]

* "Terrace Bay following liquidation process," NetNewsLedger.com, March 8, 2013. Accessed April 23, 2013. http://www.netnews-ledger.com/2013/03/08/terrace-bay-following-liquidation-process/

Web-based Branding Examples and Resources
City of Gastonia Branding Process:
http://www.cityofgastonia.com

Gastonia, North Carolina is a community of nearly 70,000, located near the larger cities of Charlotte and Winston-Salem. Because of its proximity to larger cities, Gastonia must compete with them in attracting tourism and businesses. Local community leaders have sought buy-in from the members of the community, involving all parties interested in shaping the brand image.

Establishing a Community Brand:
http://www.ourcommunity.com.au/marketing/marketing_article.jsp?articleId=1489

This article illustrates key steps in establishing a community brand, from deciding what brand to put forward through to monitoring effectiveness after the plan has been initiated. The steps provide a good checklist or starting point to the process of establishing a community brand.

Other articles with helpful tips and suggestions can be found at http://www.ourcommunity.com.au/marketing/marketing_article.jsp?articleId=1415

Ontario Tourism Brand Toolkit:
http://www.tourismpartners.com/publications/Marketing/mrktng_OTMPCBrandToolkit.pdf

This document provides information about how to make marketing strategies appealing and a breakdown of the different market segments who might want to travel to a community. As well, the document provides specific and practical advice about creating brand communications including recommendations about graphics, typeface, and layout.

Working with the Canadian Travel Trade:
http://www.tourismpartners.com/publications/Industry Resources/CanadianTravelTrade.pdf

This document, created by the Ontario Tourism Marketing Partnership Corporation (OTMPC), covers numerous topics related to establishing a community as a tourist destination, including information about how the tourism industry works, who to contact and how to design and price tourism practices. Although the guide is directed towards Northern Ontario destinations, this area shares many commonalities with many other rural areas (such as having an abundance of natural resources). The appendices at the end of the OTMPC document list websites for various organizations including governmental organizations geared towards travel and tourism as well as travel agencies, tourism operators, and suppliers that could potentially act as partners for promoting a community. Listed below are some of the websites provided in the OTMPC document.

Canadian Websites

Canadian Tourism Commission	http://www.canada.travel
Canadian Tourism Industry Exchange	http://www.canadatourismnetwork.com
Statistics Canada	http://www.statcan.gc.ca
Tourism Industry Association of Canada	http://www.tiac.travel

Ontario Websites

Ministry of Consumer Services	http://www.sse.gov.on.ca
Ontario Ministry of Tourism, Culture and Sport	http://www.mtc.gov.on.ca
Ontario Motor Coach Association	http://www.omca.com
Ontario Tourism Marketing Partnership	http://www.tourismpartners.com
Ontario Travel Information Centre	http://www.ontariotravel.net
Ontario Tourism Education Corporation	http://www.otec.org
Service Ontario	http://www.ontario.ca/serviceontario

Information for Travelers

Travel Industry Council of Ontario	http://www.tico.ca
Travel & Tourism Research Association (Canada)	http://www.ttracanada.ca

downtown core that builds on the unique qualities and architecture of this core and embraces "walkability" and the creation of inviting public spaces. Successful revitalization involves partnerships with municipal leaders, local business owners, and other community organizations.

Downtown revitalization efforts, asset-based planning, and marketing and branding initiatives are interrelated strategies for revitalizing rural communities. CED practitioners recognize that the benefits of these approaches extend beyond the individual components. Using processes that engage a broad base of community members creates a citizens' network that strengthens and supports other initiatives. It deepens civic pride resulting in a community that works together effectively to create a successful and sustainable future. Part Two provides an overview of tools and resources that assist the rural development practitioner in building successful collaborative teams.

Building Social Capital through Collaboration and Inclusiveness

A sustainable rural community "has enough economic, natural, human, and social resources to ensure it can be maintained and respond to period stresses."[1] The ability of a community to mobilize its natural and economic capital resources depends on its development and use of human and social capital. Social capital is critical for societies to prosper economically and for their development to be sustainable.

WHAT IS SOCIAL CAPITAL?

According to the World Bank, "social capital refers to the institutions, relationships, and norms that shape the quality and quantity of a society's social interactions ... Social capital is not just the sum of the institutions which underpin a society – it is the glue that holds them together." Membership in community groups of various types increases networking and economic opportunity. These networks enable collective action. In rural communities, this social fabric or infrastructure is closely linked to the economy.[2]

Social capital enhances a community's ability to work together to address common needs, foster greater inclusion and cohesion, and increase transparency and accountability. In his national bestseller *Bowling Alone*, Robert Putnam, a professor of public policy at Harvard, documented the collapse of America's social institutions. In response to the question "what can be done to reconnect society," Putnam, in partnership with Lewis Feldstein, visited

> "Many of society's complex problems require us to think beyond the divisions that caused them in the first place. The best new ideas arise when individuals and organizations work alongside others with shared values, devising multi-party or multi-sectoral strategies for social change."
>
> The Centre for Social Innovation

numerous communities where individuals and groups were engaged in unusual forms of social activism and civic renewal. From their research, the book *Better Together: Restoring the American Community* emerged along with the establishment of BetterTogether (http://www.bettertogether.org), an initiative of the Saguaro Seminar on Civic Engagement in America at Harvard University's Kennedy School of Government. Together these initiatives offer significant insight into the field of social capital. They note, social capital emphasizes "quite specific benefits that flow from the trust, reciprocity, information, and cooperation associated with social networks."[3] These social networks operate through exchanges of information, social norms of reciprocity, collective action, and solidarity between individuals and groups.

However, those in marginalized populations (e.g., youth, new immigrants, and individuals with disabilities) often lack the ability to participate fully in their communities.[4] This section, "Building Social Capital through Collaboration and Inclusiveness," highlights the potential economic benefits of social inclusion – increasing the engagement and integration of all persons into the rural business and community service sectors. Chapter 4 discusses the importance of building cross-community collaborations and offers a number of strategies for enhancing working relationships among community members. Chapter 5 explores approaches that can increase the engagement of youth in the community and economy, and reduce the out-migration of rural youth. Resources are listed to assist rural leaders seeking to build a welcoming environment that will attract and retain skilled youth. This chapter also provides insight into approaches that have successfully attracted and supported new immigrant settlement. This settlement can offer significant rural economy benefits.

4

Community Collaboration Techniques

As described in Chapter 2, creating a community asset inventory is an important step in the process to revitalize a rural economy. The community assets of talent and skills, resources and infrastructure must be linked and inter-connected to achieve real progress. This requires a shared vision and the ability to work together. *Collaboration is necessary among communities to enhance their ability to attract new economic opportunities.* Working across municipal boundaries, or with different sectors of the community (e.g., social service agencies and business), adds a layer of complexity and challenge to the process. Community leaders must understand the "art and science" of the collaborative process.

BENEFITTING FROM COMMUNITY COLLABORATION

This chapter provides guidance on how to collaborate *in a group or team-based context.* To begin, community members *need to agree to come together* as a working group. A collaborative process increases the effectiveness of new idea generation, overall project success, and social and economic change. While collaboration has the potential to be constructive, it is often a challenging process that can be characterized by conflict, a clashing of personalities, and power struggles. This is especially the case when there is a high level of interdependence among stakeholders, and when stakeholders come from diverse backgrounds.[1] Accordingly, in order for communities to fully benefit, the collaboration process must be effectively managed through the phases of idea generation, decision making and, when required, conflict management.

Community Collaboration Project (CCP) (2005–08)
http://www.brandonu.ca/rdi/

This multi-party collaboration project was initiated by the Government of Canada's Rural Secretariat. The project created a forum for various stakeholders to communicate and make decisions. In particular, this project formed a collaborative arrangement between communities in four regions of Manitoba and the Kivalliq region of Nunavut; federal, provincial, and territorial government departments and agencies; nongovernment organizations; and the Rural Development Institute (RDI) of Brandon University. The purpose of this project was to develop trusting relationships and increase communication between stakeholders as well as to explore new models of decision making and governance among communities and governments. This collaborative venture was successful because stakeholders were able to effectively work together in spite of their differing interests and agendas.

ENHANCING THE DECISION-MAKING PROCESS

Decision making is an important part of collaboration. For example, community members may decide on policies and procedures, initiatives in which to engage, and resource allocations. The following strategies can be used to create a successful and fair decision-making process.

Assign Roles and Establish the Process

The first step in a group decision-making process is to designate roles. Ideally, there should be a process manager, a timekeeper, and a recorder of information. These roles ensure that the decision-making process is organized and systematic. Designating a process manager is critical because he or she is responsible for leading and guiding the decision making process. It is recommended that the process manager follow a "rational model" of group decision making.

This classic model suggests that decision making is an integrated sequence of activities that includes (see Figure B):

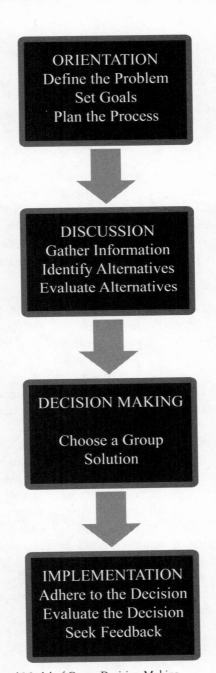

Figure B – A Rational Model of Group Decision Making

Source: Leigh Thompson, *Making the Team: A Guide for Managers* (Upper Saddle River: Pearson, 2004), 127.

a Defining the problem
b Gathering, interpreting, and exchanging information
c Choosing among alternatives
d Implementing the decision

DEFINE THE PROBLEM

After roles are assigned and a decision-making approach is agreed upon, group members must then clearly define what it is that they want to accomplish. In other words, what is the key issue(s) and what is the key decision(s) that must be reached? It is important to be explicit and clear about the goals of the process at the outset, because this will help focus subsequent discussions and ensure that they stay on track.

GATHER, INTERPRET, AND EXCHANGE INFORMATION

The group must then gather, interpret, and exchange information pertaining to the problem. Group members bring information and knowledge to the table and share their interests, concerns, and opinions. Often, group members will have conflicting viewpoints and this conflict will need to be managed effectively. Since conflict management is such an important issue in group dynamics, it will be discussed more fully below.

During this stage, the process manager acts as a facilitator and plays a critical role. He or she must ensure that there is equal participation by group members.[2] Often, one or two people do all the talking which can impede effective information exchange. The process manager can direct the discussion to suppress dominating behavior, and actively seek input from those who are saying little. The goal of this stage is to ensure that everyone's interests and concerns are voiced and addressed.

Group members should come up with a list of alternative courses of action. It is recommended that they use a whiteboard or some sort of visual aid to write out each alternative and each member's initial preferences.[3]

CHOOSE AMONG ALTERNATIVES

In choosing an alternative, as much as possible, group members should first strive for consensus. Consensus building is a process in which the discussion of the alternatives continues and all of the stakeholder's interests are continually voiced, heard, and respected.[4] This process ensures that group members gain an in-depth *understanding* of the issues with respect to each alternative. Ideally, this process will generate a high-quality agreement, one with which most stakeholders are happy.[5] If consensus building does not produce agreement, then voting (majority rule) can be used. The drawback with voting is that it can produce a low-quality agreement, one in which conflict soon reappears and stakeholders demand to revisit the entire decision-making process.

IMPLEMENT THE DECISION

To implement a decision, the group must decide who will carry out the course of action. This is particularly important in collaborations involving different levels of government. When towns, counties, and provincial/federal departments all have a hand in a decision, they may have difficulty avoiding duplication of services. To address this, a detailed list of the deliverables and tasks assigned to different individuals (or groups of individuals) should be prepared. It is vital for this to be agreed-upon and documented. After this is done, the individuals who are taking action can be held accountable; they should be responsible to keep other group members up-to-date on implementation progress and any deviations from the plan. Afterwards, if it is possible, the group should meet to evaluate the success of the decision making.

Enhancing Creativity and Idea Generation

Throughout the collaboration process, team members may need to come up with creative solutions to problems. Innovation and creativity can be fostered by using formal techniques to generate new ideas. The most common approach to idea generation is brainstorming.

BRAINSTORMING

Brainstorming is a group activity in which ideas are shared freely, without being judged or evaluated (at the outset). When conducted effectively, brainstorming can considerably increase the quality and quantity of ideas produced by group members.[6] The following rules can be applied:

- Expressiveness – No matter how strange or fanciful, group members should communicate ideas that arise. Group members should "free-wheel" whenever possible.
- Non-evaluation – Group members should withhold criticism during the idea generation phase.
- Quantity – Group members should strive for quantity of ideas, because having more ideas increases the chances of finding excellent solutions.
- Building – Group members should be encouraged to build on the ideas suggested by others whenever possible.

NOMINAL GROUP TECHNIQUE

More recent research has suggested a variation of standard brainstorming that can be extremely effective. It is the Nominal Group Technique.[7] This technique involves an initial stage of "brainwriting" – individual, written brainstorming – for about ten to fifteen minutes before the interactive brainstorming described above. Once members have come up with ideas on their own, they then share them one-by-one. The ideas are noted on a flip-chart or whiteboard. The ideas are then further discussed and clarified. The Nominal Group Technique is effective because it ensures a democratic representation of all members' ideas.

Effective Conflict Management

Conflict often arises when individuals who have differing interests and agendas make decisions together. For instance, in a community context, conflict can arise between various levels of government. When a new infrastructure project is initiated (e.g., building a road), multiple stakeholders, including local, provincial and federal governments, often share responsibilities for different aspects of the project. In this context, complex decisions about resource allocations must be made. In addition to budgetary concerns, stakeholders may disagree on which community projects should be initiated in the first place, and the timeline associated with each project.

TYPES OF CONFLICT

When one thinks of conflict, one may simply assume that it is bad and must be eliminated. However, there are some instances where conflict can be productive. Researchers have recognized two principal types of conflict, namely, *task or cognitive conflict*, and *relationship or affective conflict*.

Task conflict emerges when group members have divergent viewpoints about a task or an issue, but stay focused on solving problems caused by their differences. Relationship conflict emerges when group members attack each other personally, assign blame to each other, dislike each other because of personality clashes, and lash out emotionally.

Task conflict can be productive. This is because it can trigger discussions that force group members to analyze their problems in greater detail. This, in turn may lead to more creative thinking and overall better decision making. On the other hand, relationship conflict is associated with a decline in productivity, because it lowers the morale of the group and makes it less likely for group members to come to an agreement.[8]

CONFLICT MANAGEMENT TECHNIQUES

Community leaders can use conflict management techniques to reap the benefits of task conflict and minimize relationship conflict. Flanagan and Runde describe a number of useful actions to be taken.[9]

Create a climate of trust   In order to discuss their ideas candidly, group members must be willing to make themselves vulnerable. This means that groups need a climate of trust that allows each member to share opinions honestly and take risks without expecting to be attacked personally.[10] Such a climate is best established at the outset. Members can agree that the group is a safe place where individuals can be frank and open about ideas, and that critiques are directed at the ideas and not at individuals. This can prevent task-related discussions from degenerating into relationship conflict.

Avoid destructive behaviours   Certain behavioural tendencies in group discussions are destructive and should be avoided. They include:

- Winning at all costs – Attempting to get your way no matter what
- Avoiding – Withdrawing from the conflict altogether
- Demeaning others – Devaluing others or using sarcastic language
- Retaliating – Actively or passively trying to get even
- Hiding emotions – Concealing your true feelings.

Use constructive communication approaches   Techniques can be used to help team members cool down, slow down, and engage constructively in the face of conflict. These include:

- Self-awareness – Group members can reflect on and become aware of the kinds of situations that set them off. Being mindful of these reactions can allow group members to recognize and regulate their emotions during conflicts.
- Delay in responding – Group members can benefit from taking a brief time-out before responding to a hot issue. A brief pause can allow group members to calm down and reflect.
- Perspective taking – Group members can demonstrate that they comprehend, respect, and value the positions of other group members. They can do this by verbally acknowledging each other's points of view. This approach creates a feeling of respect even in the face of disagreements.
- Active listening – The goal of active listening is for the listener of a message to provide feedback to the sender of the message to clarify communication. The listener can do this by paraphrasing what the sender has said and by asking whether this is correct. Active listening demonstrates that the listener cares about understanding the message and allows the sender to clarify communication.[11]

SUMMARY

Harnessing the collective wisdom and energy of the full community is a powerful mechanism for revitalizing rural economies. The strategies for collaboration outlined in this chapter can be effective tools whether working within a single community or assisting with initiatives that cross multiple community boundaries. Building effective relationships begins with common goals, a solid base of trust and the desire to work together for the greater good. It is also important that community leaders ensure that their processes are inclusive – making certain that all stakeholders are invited to participate. This often requires special efforts to include young people, those new to the community, or members of the community who might be marginalized by their socioeconomic situation. The next chapter outlines approaches that ensure that youth and new Canadians are included in revitalization strategies.

Creating Community Connections through Social Enterprise – Collaboration with a Mission

Despite the efforts invested by the PRSCA (Prescott-Russell Services to Children and Adults) to assist disabled clients in finding employment, a large number of individuals still experienced chronic unemployment. Faced with this challenge, the PRSCA explored its options and the idea of creating a social enterprise emerged. After studying various models, a group of community leaders formed to discuss and evaluate the how-to of creating a new organization that would become an incubator and an operator of social businesses with a mandate to employ people at risk of chronic unemployment. For two years, this committee worked to establish exclusive agreements among various stakeholders, the PRSCA among others, and to plan the processes and procedures of this new organization.

In June 2004, Groupe Convex Prescott-Russell, http://www.groupeconvexpr.ca, was federally incorporated. Today, Convex is a not-for-profit organization, overseen by a board of directors. It acts as an umbrella organization under which social businesses are launched and operated. Groupe Convex is a network of nine social enterprises employing over one hundred people. Among these, 77 per cent are people who face serious obstacles on the job market. Most of the targeted employees live with an intellectual disability.

All of the businesses are provincially registered and belong to Groupe Convex. Profits are reinvested within the organization. One of the key benefits of this network is that the results of the individual businesses' operations are consolidated into one financial statement. Thus, even when some operations do better than others, it is the consolidated bottom line that counts the most. This structure enables new or challenged ventures to survive while reaching their mission of creating employment opportunities.

Groupe Convex has had numerous positive impacts on the community including:

- Economic – Convex allows the creation of jobs in various social enterprises. This in turn adds to the economic diversity of the community.

- Alliances – Convex has grown out of collaboration between several community agencies. This relationship encourages networking, resulting in the sharing of responsibilities, functions, and best practices. The project also enhances the ability of organizational leaders to better serve their clients, despite the fact that some face budget declines.
- Solidarity within the community – Convex has had a unifying effect in rallying leaders of organizations that are facing the same issues regarding employability and the high unemployment rate.
- Health – Convex has raised awareness about the benefits of working, specifically the importance of having disabled persons work and contribute as citizens. The employed workers are also healthier both mentally and physically.
- Educational – The project has provided a practical and concrete learning laboratory that serves as a model for rural areas across Canada, providing evidence of business solutions that can address chronic unemployment.

Groupe Convex has demonstrated social inclusion through the act of working and shown that the social economy benefits not only targeted workers, but the entire community.

Contact person: Caroline Arcand

5

Strategies for Engaging Youth and New Canadians

Rural citizens participating in 2009–2010 Southern Ontario workshops identified more than 210 community development issues and challenges and ranked them in order of importance.[1] Youth retention ranked first as leaders noted the lack of opportunities for youth which makes retaining them in the community difficult. In second place, participants ranked the combined issues of skills training, education, and literacy, recognizing the need for better access to education and advanced skills training opportunities in rural communities. Labour migration and attraction ranked eleventh. A pool of skilled workers is a key ingredient to attracting new business growth. Communities are seeking new ways to attract skilled workers. A potential resource for this skill base exists in new Canadians who bring valued technical and professional skills. Many rural communities are reaching out to new immigrants to address both the issue of skill shortages and the demographic challenges of population aging and decline. This chapter offers insight into how to remove barriers that prevent youth and new Canadians from participating fully in community revitalization.

YOUTH RETENTION AND ATTRACTION

Developing strategies that promote youth involvement and engagement is an important objective. Young people who are involved and engaged in community activities are most likely to stay in or return to their communities to take on rural careers.[2] This increases the pool of skilled workers in the community that the business community can draw on. In addition, youth participation in community activities also reduces the likelihood of their engagement in risk-associated behaviours that are harmful to the community and drain community resources.[3] Furthermore, youth who get involved in volunteer activities provide important unpaid labour for resource-strapped communities.

WHO ARE CANADA'S RURAL YOUTH AND WHAT ARE THEIR CHALLENGES?

Rural youth in Canada today face a number of challenges that are not shared with their urban counterparts. These challenges result in youth outmigration to urban centres.

1 Transportation – Because many rural areas do not have public transportation systems, residents must rely on other forms of transportation. Due to the longer distances involved in rural commuting, walking and bicycling are usually not viable options, leaving automobiles as the main alternative. This poses a number of problems for youth who generally do not own vehicles. They may not be able to participate in social activities (e.g., movies, shopping, sports, dances, and community centre activities) to the degree they wish. As well, they may not be able to access or carry out certain jobs because of transportation limitations.
2 Socializing/Extracurricular – Non work-related activities are an important part of all of our lives. Many youth feel that their communities do not offer them sufficient extra-curricular activities or social/cultural activities. The social/cultural infrastructure may be geared towards the very young or retirees.
3 Employment – Rural individuals aged 20–29 experience lower employment rates than urban youth. In addition, more blue-collar and fewer professional and managerial positions are available.
4 Education – A lack of local education opportunities for youth may limit their potential to develop skills and abilities to be competitive in local, regional, and national economies. There may be minimal or no post-secondary education institutions in their communities, limited availability of adult education, lack of on-the-job training opportunities, and lack of local training and education programs to help develop entrepreneurial skills.

Considering these challenges it is no wonder that studies show that more than half of rural youth intend to move to more urban centres. Overall, those most likely to move out of rural areas are relatively young, are not married, have a university degree, and have had limited success in the labour market. Research shows that only about a third of former rural youth who live in urban centres intend to return to their rural communities. How then do rural communities retain current local youth and attract youth living in urban centres? They must connect them to the community.

FOCUSING ON KEY PRINCIPLES AND VALUES

How are connections to communities made? Below are basic principles and values that can guide decision making about youth retention planning:

1 Engagement – Youth must feel engaged. This means encouraging them and providing them with opportunities to be active in their communities. Engagement is created by appealing to their interests and giving them something to be passionate about.
2 Participation – Youth should be solicited for their advice, input, feelings, ideas etc. in various aspects of community functioning. Creating solid buy-in and a sense of ownership through participatory approaches to community decision making will also increase their motivation and sense of belonging. It will make youth feel they are valued members of their community.
3 Leadership – Connections cannot be made without meaningful integration. Not only should youth participate in community planning of their own retention, but they should be given opportunities to occupy various community leadership roles. This also will create a sense of ownership and worth.

RETENTION STRATEGIES AND TACTICS

Many of the suggestions below come from youth themselves.

1 Transportation
   a Improve bike lanes so that bicycling is at least an option.
   b Create car co-ops that organize a method of vehicle sharing.

    c Organize special events buses that go to events in other rural areas and also to urban centres.

    d Use school buses more efficiently. Give youth more bus options so that they can use these buses to get to jobs and friends' houses. Provide later buses that allow students to stay at school for sports and other activities.

2 Socializing/Extra Curricular Activities

    a Encourage the development of cultural and social events directed at youth.

    b Provide youth the opportunity to organize events themselves.

3 Employment

    a Develop youth mentoring and apprenticeship programs that partner with local businesses.

    b Have employers designate some positions as 'youth only' to facilitate the entry of youth into rural careers. This may include subsidizing youth wages.

    c Provide entrepreneurship training that will help youth start their own local businesses.

    d Hold local business plan competitions and assist the winners.

    e Help local businesses create summer employment programs to maintain connections with youth who have left to attend post-secondary institutions. This may include subsidizing youth wages.

4 Education

    a Create career training programs in high schools to ensure youth are familiar with rural career options and know how to position themselves to stay in their communities and still reach their desired levels of career success.

    b Create co-operative education programs that partner with local business and industry.

    c Encourage distance education by informing youth of opportunities, and also by providing necessary support such as Internet access. Promote group enrollment in distance programs to facilitate the development of support networks. Offer facilities where youth can meet for studying and discussion.

5 Leadership

    a Organize a youth advisory committee.

    b Create community youth leadership positions, for example, in a civic affairs committee.

c Facilitate the creation of a youth-led local newspaper or newsletter. This could publicize youth accomplishments, opportunities, activities, etc.

HOW CAN YOUTH BE ENGAGED IN THE COMMUNITY?

Three strategies community leaders in rural areas can use to promote youth involvement and engagement are:

• Facilitating the development of community programs
• Promoting youth leadership
• Communicating opportunities to youth

Facilitating the Development of Community Programs

Community programs provide the means for youth to participate in constructive activities outside their schools and families. Community programs include after-school events, extracurricular activities, youth clubs, and youth development programs.

Typically, community programs are associated with sports or arts-related initiatives; however, many other programming possibilities exist including skills-based programs, academic-support programs, and leadership development programs. Diversity in community programs is advantageous because a wider range of individual interests and needs will be met. Put simply, more youth will be involved.

There is also diversity in the organizations that offer community programs. These organizations include faith-based institutions, schools, libraries, hospitals, community centres, sports organizations, arts and cultural organizations, and national agencies such as Boys and Girls Clubs, 4H, and Scouts Canada. Also, individuals such as community, spiritual, or youth leaders may also initiate programs.[4]

Accordingly, community economic development (CED) practitioners should recognize:

• The diversity in the types of programs that a community can offer
• The value in offering a diverse set of community programs
• The diversity in the kinds of organizations and individuals available to coordinate community programs

To facilitate the development of programs, CED professionals can be proactive by approaching organizations and individuals who are well positioned to organize programs. Recognizing diversity (as mentioned above) is key, because it allows community leaders to be creative.

Furthermore, programs need to be supported financially. Communities can do this by directly sponsoring programs and/or making program organizers aware of organizations that fund community projects for youth, for example through grants. (See Appendix B for a list of some of these organizations.) CED practitioners can offer to work with program organizers to develop high-quality grant applications. Alternatively, they can identify others in the community who are skilled in writing grants who may be able to help program organizers apply for funding. (See Appendix B for resources to assist with the development of youth programming.)

Promoting Youth Leadership

As described earlier, youth become more engaged in the community when they have opportunities to take on leadership roles. Youth are more likely to take on such roles when:

· Opportunities exist to participate in community decisions
· Role models in the community exist and are visible

Visibility and voice empower youth, give them a sense of responsibility, and develop them to be the leaders of the future.[5] Communities benefit because youth are enthusiastic, energetic, and bring fresh and unique perspectives to the table.

One way youth can be included in decision-making processes is through the establishment of youth cabinets. They draw together young leaders to discuss community issues and organize community initiatives. For example, Toronto has a Youth Cabinet to advise City Council,[6] the City of Vaughan has a Youth Cabinet,[7] and in a rural setting, several hospital foundations on Prince Edward Island have established youth boards.[8]

When initiating a youth cabinet, a community leader will initially need to take ownership of the project. He or she must find youth interested in serving as cabinet members. A good place to start is to approach local high schools and network with teachers and students. In most cases, membership should be open. Once members have joined, the cabinet should designate executives of the cabinet, usually youth, who chair the discussion in meetings, coordinate meeting times, and lead any proposed initiatives.

It is important to note that it is not simply enough for youth to meet and discuss issues. For youth to feel empowered their voice needs to be heard; this necessitates a link between the youth cabinet and community leaders (e.g., city/town committees and councillors). As such, community leaders need to be open to having youth present at their meetings so that their ideas and opinions can be discussed. City and town councils can establish policies to include youth as required members of consultative projects.

Furthermore, for this collaboration to be successful, adult community leaders need to demonstrate they take youth seriously.[9] For example, they should be seen to be listening to youth and validating their ideas. Providing validation does not mean automatically agreeing. Adults are expected to provide comments and constructive criticism. Adult leaders need to encourage and authorize youth to take action and implement their plans.

Another way that community leaders can promote youth leadership is to recognize youth leaders for their achievements and to make them visible in the community. Recognizing the accomplishments of rural youth can motivate others to become involved and engaged. Awards can be established for youth who have demonstrated outstanding leadership and community service. For example, some rural communities offer not only a citizen of the year award, but also a youth citizen of the year award.[10] Other types of awards can be given to youth who initiate and lead community programs. It is essential for awards to be made public so that other youth can be aware of their peers' activities. Local newspapers can be invited to cover awards ceremonies.

Finally, youth who are interested in entrepreneurship can be mentored by members of the business community. Mentorship helps to provide the skills and experience necessary to become business leaders of the future. It increases the chances that youth will stay in the community to work in the business sector. Youth may choose to work for a business where they received a mentorship opportunity, or they may start their own local business. Community leaders should identify members of the business community who can volunteer as mentors.

Communicating Opportunities

Community programs and leadership opportunities may be in place, but youth cannot participate if they are not aware that these opportunities exist. It is therefore essential that CED professionals effectively communicate opportunities to youth. They should raise awareness of:

- Community programs that are available to youth
- Volunteer opportunities
- Awards for youth leadership

Today's youth increasingly use technology to communicate and learn about what is going on around them. Specifically, online social networking tools, such as Facebook, have become very popular. On Facebook, people can create personal profiles that contain information about themselves (e.g., personal information, their interests, their opinions, what they are doing, and events they are attending). These profiles can be viewed by friends, and provide information on what events are happening in a community.

Communication using social networking technologies like Facebook is the way of the future.[11] Community leaders can take advantage of this communication medium to advertise opportunities, events, and programs. For example, an organization that collects data on volunteer opportunities could create a Facebook profile of what they do, and post a list of all volunteer opportunities. Then, they could send invitations to youth in the community to view this profile. To do this effectively, community leaders need to be trained on how to create and update a Facebook profile.[12]

In addition to using social media, community leaders can post youth-related information and opportunities on one or more community websites. As an example, Volunteer & Information Kingston is an organization that coordinates volunteer work and has a website with a volunteer database.[13]

Not all rural communities will have access to broadband Internet services. In such cases, community leaders will need to rely on more traditional communication methods. Community leaders can visit places where youth frequent and advertise using posters on bulletin boards. They can also talk to other leaders (e.g., teachers, coaches, spiritual leaders, parents) and spread the word about youth opportunities. Word-of-mouth advertising can be effective, especially in rural communities that are tightly knit.

High school students in Ontario are required to complete a minimum of 40 hours of community service.[14] As such, it would be worthwhile for rural Ontario community leaders to communicate volunteer opportunities in high schools, so that teachers and guidance counselors could readily spread the word.

ENGAGING NEW CANADIANS

Also important for rural population sustainability, regional economic development, and cultural vitality are the attraction and engagement of new Canadians.[15] Immigrants can help businesses address labour shortages, provide professional services that are in demand (e.g., those offered by physicians and other healthcare professionals), and create jobs as entrepreneurs. An influx of immigrants can help communities deal with population decline due to youth out-migration. Historically, however, the distribution of immigrants in Canada has been concentrated in major cities, notably Toronto, Montreal, and Vancouver, and smaller rural municipalities have not been as successful in attracting new arrivals.[16] As such, it is imperative that rural CED practitioners adopt strategies to attract immigrants to their communities. The experiences of Winkler, Manitoba highlight a community's success in attracting and integrating immigrants into its community life and economy.

PLANNING AN ENGAGEMENT STRATEGY

The following key steps can assist community leaders in implementing an attraction and engagement plan for new Canadians.

It Begins with a Committee

A committee should be formed to develop, coordinate, and implement immigrant attraction strategies. This committee should include designates from immigrant-serving agencies as well as representatives from key sectors including business, education, health, housing and recreation.[17] Each member can serve as a champion for immigration and must be convinced of the value of attracting immigrants and ensuring that the community benefits from immigration.[18]

Winkler, MB

The City of Winkler in Manitoba has been very successful in attracting immigrants to grow its local economy and address its human resource needs. Although the community is rural with a population of roughly 8,500, its population grew by approximately 3,325 between 1999 and 2006 through immigration. This strong immigration was made possible by a buoyant economy, mostly in the agricultural sector. Additionally, many of the employers who provided jobs in this period made use of the Provincial Nominee Program which began in 1998.

The group of new arrivals in Winkler included predominantly Russian-Germans and Germans. Once a critical mass of new immigrants arrived in Winkler, they provided information to other prospective immigrants through word of mouth, highlighting Winkler as an attractive and desirable place to live. For many immigrants, Winkler has offered German linguistic and religious linkages.

To facilitate immigration integration, the Chamber of Commerce formed an Immigration Integration Committee soon after the first group of immigrants arrived. This committee became the main community contact for immigration concerns and took a keen interest in working with the province to assist arriving immigrants and address their settlement needs. Specifically, Winkler organized settlement and language services through the South Central Settlement and Employment Services (SCSES) and the Pembina Valley Language Education for Adults (PVLEA). A new office of SCSES was opened in November 2004, centralizing settlement, employment, and English as a Second Language services in one location. Additional assistance offered included providing connections to vital services, offering language interpretation, and providing information about life in Central Manitoba and Canada. Standardized settlement services, as well as those designed to meet individualized needs, were provided.

Of all the services, language instruction was regarded as particularly important. New immigrants' inability to understand and communicate in English was a major limiting factor for effective integration into the community and subsequent employment. Accordingly, PVLEA was founded to provide literacy and English as a Second Language classes for new immigrants. Funded by the province of Manitoba, the community language program accommodated 300 adult students using fifteen instructors.

In addition to the services provided by the community, immigrants also found great comfort and support from previously settled immigrants. For instance, the Mennonite Central Committee and Church Elders assisted in immigrant integration, underscoring the important role that religious institutions can play in supporting newcomers. It has been observed that immigrants who left the community generally did not have a strong affiliation with a church or with other local immigrants.

Winkler is an example of how a community can attract a large number of new Canadians to its area and integrate them effectively into the community. In particular, a community needs to have employment opportunities available for newcomers. Employers can make use of the Provincial Nominee Program to enable immigration. Also, the settlement services described play a pivotal role in integrating newcomers. Last, the existing immigrant community and religious institutions can provide critical support.

Marketing and Promoting the Community

CED professionals must promote the positive attributes of the community. Immigrants will choose where to settle based on economic and social strengths that make the community an attractive destination. These strengths needed to be communicated effectively and can be done so in the following ways.

A COMMUNITY WEBSITE FOR IMMIGRANTS

One of the most important initiatives that a community can take on to attract immigrants is the creation of a community website designed specifically for immigrants. A website is readily accessible, can be created with a low budget, and is able to communicate information over great distances. To assist communities in the past,

Durham Immigration Portal
http://www.durhamimmigration.ca
  The Region of Durham encompasses eight municipalities east of Toronto. This region, composed of both urban and rural communities, is expecting to grow from its 2001 population of 531,000 to 970,000 by 2021. Its economic plan is built on the development of a skilled workforce through attracting newcomers.
  As part of this strategy, the region established an online immigration portal to connect immigrants with social, health, and employment resources. Additionally, the community established the Durham Region Diversity and Immigration Partnership Council to help foster a welcoming environment for people from all walks of life. Already, the community has seen the signs of growing diversity through the establishment of new places of worship, businesses, and activities that reflect a variety of cultures.

the Government of Ontario has allocated funds for the creation of online resources geared towards immigrants. Helpful resources for community leaders to use when designing new websites are listed in Appendix C.

VISITS TO THE AREA
CED practitioners can encourage prospective immigrants to visit the area, offering them first-hand knowledge and an accurate impression of what it is like to live locally. Immigrants' assumptions of rural life may differ dramatically from the reality of many rural communities. During the visits, community representatives should try to communicate the positive experiences of immigrants who have already settled in the area. Positive word of mouth from settled immigrants supports the notion that the community is a good place in which to live and work.

IMMIGRANT NETWORKS
Community leaders should try to tap into immigrants' established social networks to facilitate information flows to friends, relatives,

and business partners. This can increase the community's visibility overseas.

OVERSEAS EVENTS
Some communities have the budget to actually travel to overseas jobs and emigration fairs to promote their area.[19] While this is an expensive option, it can be effective in recruiting new immigrants from a particular region. At these fairs, it is critical that the kinds of economic opportunities that are available in the community are presented and that prospective immigrants can be put in touch with potential employers.

Attracting Immigrant Entrepreneurs

Immigrant entrepreneurs are valuable because they can potentially create new jobs and spur economic growth. As such, CED professionals must do all they can to profile their communities as good places to start businesses. For instance, they can highlight the fact that operating costs may be lower in rural areas, and provide information on the types of services in their areas that can help entrepreneurs succeed (e.g., business incubators and professional services).

Creating a Welcoming Community

To attract immigrants, it is essential for communities to engage in initiatives that signal that they welcome new arrivals.[20] A welcoming community that integrates its immigrants well gains a positive reputation and attracts more immigrants. Community leaders can create a welcoming environment in the following ways.

COMMUNICATING THE BENEFITS OF IMMIGRATION
A community's current residents and businesses will be more receptive to immigrants if they understand the benefits that immigrants bring.[21] Immigrants are valuable to the economic growth and cultural diversity of a community. Negative stereotypes of immigrants need to be resisted and opposed. For instance, in North Bay, this has been done effectively through positive portrayals of local immigrants in the media and through a diversity awareness program.[22]

PROVIDING SETTLEMENT SERVICES

Community settlement services are essential in helping immigrants to effectively integrate into the community. Some settlement services that communities offer include:[23]

- Information and orientation about life in the community
- Language interpretation
- Information about healthcare, education, banking, law, shopping, housing, etc.
- Connection to community services (doctors, dentists, schools, etc.)
- Connection to English as a Second Language (ESL) classes
- Employment assistance

CELEBRATING ETHNIC HERITAGE IN THE COMMUNITY

A community can welcome immigrants by celebrating ethnic heritage and multiculturalism.[24] It can do this by increasing efforts to incorporate multicultural celebrations into community events. For example, as part of its Canada Day celebration, Barrhaven held a Multicultural Festival to recognize the different ethnic groups in the area. These kinds of events symbolize to community members that multiculturalism is valued in the community.

Applying to Government Programs

Government programs exist that: (1) facilitate the process of immigration to rural communities, and (2) provide the monetary resources to create programs that attract, integrate, and support immigrants. Such funding can help municipalities with limited resources to expand their capacity to draw on the talents, skills, and contributions of newcomers to Canada. Appendix C lists a number of municipalities that have developed newcomer websites, and Appendix D provides details on government funding sources.

SUMMARY

Rural communities facing demographic shifts and depopulation need to consider new strategies to retain their current citizens and attract new residents and businesses. The CED practitioner plays several roles ranging from acting as information broker to connecting local champions with other successful community leaders.

In the area of youth retention, CED professionals should assist community leaders in their efforts to engage young people in the processes and decisions that shape the community. Mentoring programs for young entrepreneurs and the inclusion of youth in community processes that relate to economic revitalization are two specific approaches that can ensure the youth voice is heard. At the same time, CED practitioners should examine and address barriers that might prohibit young people from fully participating in the local economy such as access to transportation and training opportunities.

Similarly, these economic development professionals can encourage municipal leaders to develop plans to attract new Canadians. Several rural communities have been leading efforts in this area and have initiated successful immigration attraction strategies. Linking to these communities builds the capacity of local leaders to understand the potential processes and impacts of encouraging new settlement.

PART THREE

New Options for Growing the Rural Economy

The creative economy is an important economic driver for rural communities. In addition to stimulating innovations, the knowledge-based economy is influencing traditional employment in the resource and manufacturing sectors. Technology is being utilized in new ways and traditional products are being modified by value-added processes. New technologies also require new or enhanced skill bases for employees. All this creates new rural economy dynamics and fosters entrepreneurial businesses.

Small businesses and the jobs they create are critical for vibrant rural economies. The Canadian Federation of Independent Business reports that small and medium-sized enterprises (SMEs) employ about 53 per cent of all working individuals in Canada today.[1] Further:

- 80 per cent of all new jobs come from small and medium-sized firms
- 41 per cent of the total private sector workforce works in enterprises of fewer than twenty employees[2]
- 45 per cent of Canada's GDP is generated by small and mid-sized businesses (under 500 employees).[3]

These same businesses play an integral part in the economic and social well-being of communities. Finding strategies to support the development and growth of these local businesses, especially those related to the creative economy, was identified as a key research priority by community leaders in the 2009–2010 Monieson Centre Discovery Workshop series. In particular, leaders asked:

- Do innovative rural businesses have unique needs?
- Are there lessons to be learned from how these businesses overcame challenges associated with establishing and growing their
  operations?
- What additional support could rural municipal leaders provide
  to help these businesses survive and thrive?

The case studies, Wild Wing, The Green Beaver Company,
Whistlestop Productions, Pefferlaw Peat Products, Fifth Town
Artisan Cheese, and Ontario Water Buffalo Company, in the following chapters represent a cross-section of innovative businesses
contributing to Eastern Ontario's economic growth. Fourth-year
business policy students at Queen's School of Business interviewed
a total of eighteen successful rural business entrepreneurs, identified by the Eastern Ontario CFDC Network, Inc. The CFDCs were a
significant source of start-up or expansion financing for the majority of the businesses identified. These studies highlight innovative practices as well as operational strategies – both in place and
planned – that are helping the businesses grow in a changing rural
economic context. In addition to the cases presented here, the complete series is available on the Monieson Centre's economic revitalization online portal at http://www.easternontarioknowledge.ca
or at http://business.queensu.ca/centres/monieson/economic_
revitalization/.

Over the last decade, the work of Richard Florida on the creative
economy has captured the attention of policy-makers and stimulated vibrant debate in academic research. At the heart of Florida's
creative economy tenets is the argument that economic growth is
now dependent on the talent of a *creative class* who innovate and
produce ideas, new technologies, and/or creative output.[4] The creative economy is an evolving concept based on creative assets that
can generate economic growth. While there is no single, agreed-
upon definition for the creative economy and no unique classifica-
tion of the creative industries, the United Nations Conference on
Trade and Development (UNCTAD) outlines the following param-
eters for the creative economy:[5]

- It can foster income generation, job creation, and export earnings
  while promoting social inclusion, cultural diversity and human
  development.

"Prince Edward County is well known for its creative economy which employs over 30% of the local labour force, pays 46% of the wages and accounts for 60% of disposable income, and is expected to grow by 40% over the next decade."

Dan Taylor, former economic development officer,
Prince Edward County

- It embraces economic, cultural, and social aspects interacting with technology, intellectual property and tourism objectives.
- It is a set of knowledge-based economic activities with a development dimension and cross-cutting linkages at macro and micro levels to the overall economy.

Historically, the economy of most rural regions began with or was closely linked to either a resource base such as agriculture or forestry or to an industrial and manufacturing base often built on nearby natural resources. The introduction of new technologies, demographic shifts, and the move towards a more global market perspective had a significant impact on the traditional economic drivers that were the source of prosperity for many rural communities. Rural communities faced with an aging population, youth out-migration, and the closure of industries and small business have been challenged by the resulting loss of tax base and fewer opportunities for employment.

At the same time, a growing number of municipalities have been experiencing an influx of new residents. Newly retired professionals are being joined by young families seeking the quality of place and access to cultural and natural amenities that small rural communities offer. This rejuvenation is supported by advances in telecommunications connectivity that have created new business opportunities, greater access of rural residents to educational resources, and increased information and awareness about the potential of the creative economy.

A 2009 report by Millier Dickinson Blais, AuthentiCity, Dr. Greg Spencer, and the Martin Prosperity Institute[6] details the successes and challenges of a region aiming to grow its creative economy.

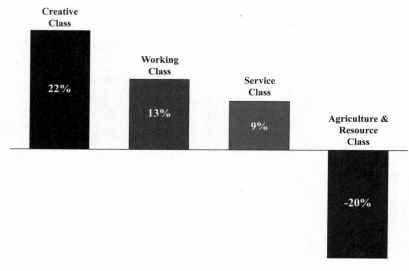

Figure C – Rural Ontario Job Growth, 1996–2006

Source: "Creativity in the Rural Economy: Opportunities in Rural Areas & Smaller Centres," *Martin Prosperity Institute*, September 23, 2009. Accessed Aug. 31, 2011 http://www.martinprosperity.org/insights/insight/creativity-in-the-rural-economy-opportunities-in-rural-areas-smaller-centres

It shows that job growth in rural Ontario in the decade between 1996 and 2006 was led by creative class workers at 22 per cent – ahead of the working class at 13 per cent, the service class at 9 per cent and the agricultural and resource class, where the number of jobs actually fell by 20 per cent.

Why does the creative economy matter to rural communities? There are at least two important reasons. First, a high proportion of creative class jobs – high-autonomy occupations in which workers are paid to think like managers, scientists, and designers – can be linked to higher wages and economic growth. Second, creativity is important to all industries. While some members of the creative class work in creative industries like web design or music, most work in more traditional industries like manufacturing or agriculture, adding value through creative problem solving and innovation. Community economic development (CED) practitioners can play significant roles in supporting entrepreneurs and their businesses.

6

Supporting the "Creative Class" and Entrepreneurs

WHAT IS "THE CREATIVE CLASS"?

The creative class is made up of individuals employed in "science, engineering, arts, culture, entertainment, and the knowledge-based professions of management, finance, law, healthcare, and education."[1] Richard Florida and his contemporaries argue that the creative class flourishes in places that offer the "Three Ts" of economic development – Talent, Tolerance, and Technology[2] – as well as a wide range of natural, cultural, and recreational amenities. This has translated into economic development strategies aimed at encouraging innovation, attracting highly-skilled workers, and promoting quality of place. Urban design features like street-scaping along with vibrant downtowns and an arts and culture scene are argued to be crucial in attracting and retaining these talented individuals. Equally important are access to top-notch post-secondary institutions, public transit, quality affordable housing, museums, and natural amenities like parks and paths that offer leisure opportunities.[3]

The creative economy literature has spawned a number of debates. These include discussing whether skilled workers relocate for amenities, tolerance, and diversity – three markers of the creative class – or in order to maximize job opportunities.[4] Simply put, do jobs follow people or do people follow jobs? Another dispute arises over creating policies that are shaped more by the perceived preferences of skilled professionals from outside a community than by the preferences of current residents.[5] A particular concern for rural communities is the urban focus of much creative economy research. The creative economy literature is based mainly on studies of large cities and the resulting economic development strategies are focused on urban policy insights.[6]

Despite these debates, few dispute the creative economy literature's emphasis on the importance of human capital and quality of place. Many rural areas are turning to the creative economy to combat economic uncertainty and attract talented individuals. However, the creative economy functions differently in different rural areas; creative economic development strategies are not one-size-fits-all.[7]

THE RURAL CREATIVE ECONOMY

Although the rural creative economy has only recently attracted attention in academic research, it is commonly argued that rural areas have many of the place-based amenities that attract creative workers. For example, Kevin Stolarick and colleagues from the Martin Prosperity Institute at the University of Toronto state that "[m]any of the qualities cities so often try to replicate in order to attract the creative class, such as heightened quality of place, local pristine natural amenities and unique cultural and heritage opportunities, exist in abundance in rural communities."[8] They suggest that place-based marketing tactics often used to attract tourists can also be applied to attracting the creative class.

A recent paper by Bell and Jayne examines the creative countryside and rural cultural industries in the United Kingdom.[9] They argue that policymakers need to avoid overlaying urban creative policies in rural areas that are often based on sectors perceived to be part of the rural idyll like arts and crafts. They have also discovered a tension between creative industries located in rural areas and their urban counterparts. Often creative industries in rural areas are seen as hobbies, i.e., low quality and parochial, whereas urban creative industries are seen as innovative and high-end. To attract talented individuals, they stress the importance of lifestyle migration for rural amenities but also economic arguments including affordability. Overall, they document the rising advocacy for a rural cultural strategy in the UK where arts and culture are used to promote employment, economic development, and regeneration.

In their work on American rural counties, McGranahan and Wojan discover that employment in creative occupations is linked with employment growth in rural areas.[10] The authors also find that the rural creative class is older and more likely to be married. Economic development strategies geared at improving the quality of local schools may be more critical in rural areas rather than creating hip downtowns with chic cafés. The authors suggest that rurality itself is the main driver as people give up urban amenities for the natural amenities and quality of life found in rural areas. However, they stress that not all rural areas can attract the creative class. Location, natural amenities, adequate density, a reasonable level of services, and commuting potential are all important in the rural creative economy.

In her work on artists in American rural areas, Markusen argues that artists contribute to the consumption base of a local economy.[11] For example, performances, art displays, and readings of written work can produce modest growth in local income. Plus, many rural areas have underutilized infrastructure like closed theatres and abandoned buildings that can be revitalized to serve as housing, studio space, gallery space, or performance space. She also believes that artists are attracted to rural areas because of the affordability, vintage architecture, quiet, and sense of community. In their work in Canadian rural areas, Mitchell, Bunting, and Piccioni agree that rural communities offer advantages for visual artists in terms of creativity. They discover for many artists, "the landscape provides the raw materials (i.e., subject matter) for the creative process."[12] Markusen suggests occupational targeting focused on artists as a possible rural economic development strategy.

PRINCE EDWARD COUNTY – ARGUABLY CANADA'S FIRST CREATIVE RURAL ECONOMY

Prince Edward County (PEC) is an island rural community in eastern Ontario. It is located in the heart of Canada's Creative Corridor – a "megaregion" between Toronto, Ottawa, and Montreal that represents 50 per cent of Canada's GDP.[13] This location provides PEC with many creative economy growth opportunities. In 2006, the population was 25,496; however, the median age for PEC was 47.7 compared to 39.0 for Ontario.[14] In their report, Stolarick et al. find that PEC has a higher percentage of its population between twenty-five and sixty-four with a university degree than other areas in the province that are outside a major urban region (17.2% and 12.3% respectively).[15] They also find that the percentage of workers in creative occupations rose in PEC from 24.3% in 1996 to 30.9% in 2006, compared to 23.5% and 26.0% for other areas in the province that are outside a major urban region.

Agriculture has a long history in PEC, which was settled over 200 years ago by United Empire Loyalists fleeing the United States during the American Revolution. The dominant agricultural sectors include dairy, beef, and grains and oilseeds.[16] However, as Donald argues, Prince Edward County is at the forefront of Ontario's new creative food movement.[17] In fact, PEC is quickly becoming one of Canada's fastest growing wine regions and it is Ontario's fourth Designated Viticultural Area (DVA). In less than a decade, PEC's land use has gone from less than twenty acres of vines to more than 600 acres, with almost a dozen wineries attracting over $30 million in investment.[18] Tourism also plays a significant role in the PEC economy, drawing traditionally on its natural amenities including Sandbanks Provincial Park.[19] The creative food movement, however, has diversified the county's tourism. The *quality of taste* is celebrated in the area through initiatives like the annual TASTE! food and wine event which showcases local cuisine.[20]

Over the last decade, PEC has led an aggressive strategy to attract educated and creative workers to the area. The County has capitalized on the place-based amenities that make the area unique. For example, PEC is fortunate to have over 800 km of coastline[21] on the shores of Lake Ontario and vintage architecture with a long history. With this rich quality of life, PEC has attracted many "escape artists," creative professionals who desire to leave the city to work and live in rural areas.[22] PEC is already home to over a hundred independent artists and galleries complemented by artistic institutions like the Regent Theatre and an annual Jazz Festival.[23] The County also uses an aesthetically pleasing website, http://www.buildanewlife.ca, to attract creative investment. PEC has further recognized the importance of industry clustering in the creative economy through the Taste Trail. This involves strategic partnerships and co-marketing between farms, cheese producers, wineries, breweries, and restaurants in the County.[24] As arguably Canada's first creative rural economy,[25] Prince Edward County is well positioned to take advantage of the new creative food movement and attract and retain creative professionals.

POLICY INSIGHTS FOR HARVESTING A RURAL CREATIVE ECONOMY

Not all rural areas can attract the creative class or harvest a rural creative economy. As outlined earlier, location, commutability, natural amenities, adequate density, and the availability of a reasonable level of services are important. That being said, there are a number of general strategies that can help promote creative economic development in rural areas:

- A Strategic Plan – Start with an economic development plan outlining key goals and strategies.
- SWOT Analysis – Be realistic and acknowledge community Strengths, Weaknesses, Opportunities, and Threats.
- "Joined-up Governance" – Embrace a popular concept in the United Kingdom which encourages all levels of government to work together towards a common goal.

To combat economic uncertainty in rural America, Morgan, Lambe and Freyer suggest three specific strategies:[26]

- Place-based Development – Economic Development strategies should capitalize on distinct qualities of place including natural amenities and cultural or historic traditions.
- Economic Gardening – Focus on growing entrepreneurs and providing a healthy environment for small business growth.
- Cultivating Creativity and Talent – Recognize the importance of attracting and retaining creative professionals and industries.

To grow a creative countryside, Bell and Jayne offer the following suggestions:[27]

- "Greentrification" – Combine traditional and new materials, techniques, and uses to build a new rural aesthetic. For example, consider barn conversions, art farms, maize mazes, promoting local food and drink movements, and promoting the creative benefits of rural living.
- Cross-Marketing – Develop promotions and marketing initiatives across sectors that may seem distinct, like tourism, food and drink, and cultural production.

Bell and Jayne's interviews with creative professionals also identified that showcasing events, networking opportunities, exhibition space, and access to high-tech equipment like broadband are important support strategies in which rural communities should invest.[28] Markusen also suggests investing in space for artists like performance spaces, live/work spaces, and artists' centres.[29] One final suggestion to help grow a rural creative economy includes creating industry clusters using tools like entrepreneurial incubators. Michael Porter defines clusters as "geographic concentrations of interconnected companies, specialized suppliers and service providers, firms in related industries, and associated institutions (e.g., universities, standards agencies, and trade associations) in particular fields that compete but also cooperate."[30] Roger Martin and Richard Florida, in their report Ontario in the Creative Age, emphasize the importance of clustering industry and talent in the creative economy.[31]

However, rural areas looking to the creative economy need to be aware of challenges that might arise. These include rural gentrification, which can result in soaring house prices and make it difficult to maintain and protect the quality of life that made the region attractive to begin with.[32] Tensions can also arise between current residents who value old traditions and creative professionals with new ideas. An equally significant challenge can be the need for clustering and agglomeration in the creative economy; industry and talent clustering may not be possible in rural areas that lack density and proximity to mega regions.[33]

CREATING AN ENTREPRENEURIAL CLIMATE

The innovation and idea sharing found in a vibrant creative economy are also common to communities that support entrepreneurship and new business ventures. Fostering entrepreneurship can drastically improve the well-being and quality of life in rural communities. Entrepreneurship creates jobs for community members, wealth for business owners, and helps rural communities become independent, self-sustaining, and prosperous. "Home grown" enterprises in rural communities are likely to remain loyal to the place in which they were developed and will export their goods and services outside the local region fostering economic growth within the community.[34] To foster entrepreneurship, communities need to provide assistance to entrepreneurs in order to support the creation, growth, and survival of their businesses. Community leaders need to collaborate to engage in effective practices that foster entrepreneurship. Communities that are entrepreneurial do the following:

- Provide financial incentives to entrepreneurs and investors
- Provide valuable business information to entrepreneurs
- Develop the skills of entrepreneurs
- Create networking opportunities for entrepreneurs

FINANCIAL INCENTIVES

Communities can foster entrepreneurship by advocating that various levels of governments offer tax relief to small business entrepreneurs and investors. For instance, the government of Yukon has created the Yukon Small Business Investment Tax Credit which is a personal tax credit that reduces income tax for investors who invest in eligible businesses.[35] Likewise, the province of Manitoba offers a number of tax credits for entrepreneurs who start businesses built upon new and innovative technologies across all industry sectors.[36] At a more local level, the County of Douglas-Coffee in Georgia offers tax abatements to small business entrepreneurs.[37] These incentives promote entrepreneurship by reducing financial challenges and risks. They make investing in a start-up potentially more profitable than investing in an established business.

Another way communities can help entrepreneurs reduce costs is by developing a business incubator in the region. Business incubators accelerate the development of start-up companies. Incubator buildings are generally occupied by several start-up businesses at the same time. Incubators are financially attractive to entrepreneurs because they typically provide rents below market rates. In addition, they provide, for a very modest fee (often on a per use basis), shared administrative and technical services (e.g., reception, clerical assistance, Internet access, and technical support).

Recent research suggests that business incubators can be very effective in helping entrepreneurs start, develop, and succeed in their business ventures.[38] In addition to providing financial incentives, business incubators provide business assistance services such as business basics, accounting/financial management, and marketing assistance that help develop the skills of the entrepreneurs. Also, since business incubators house many different companies at one point in

Case Study – Wild Wing Restaurants

Company Overview and Background

The first Wild Wing opened its doors on March 17, 1999 in the small town of Sunderland, Ontario. Founder Rick Smiciklas conceived the idea for the restaurant only two months earlier, and, with an initial $600 loan from a family member and a $15,000 bank loan, started a unique business: a restaurant specializing in chicken wings. Today, twelve years later, Wild Wing Restaurants is a Canadian franchised family restaurant chain serving 101 varieties of chicken wings at more than sixty locations across Ontario.

The philosophy of the business revolves around offering a creative menu, high-quality food and customer service, as well as a unique dining atmosphere. The business creates a memorable experience by designing each restaurant to resemble an old-time saloon with pine floors and walls covered in chicken wire. All Wild Wing restaurants are locally owned and operated by people passionate about making a difference and supporting their communities.

Success Factors

Wild Wing's success has led to a significant amount of growth over a relatively short period of time. Their success stems from three major factors:

1 Differentiated Product Offering

Wild Wing's central distinguishing factor is also a primary reason for its success. By being one of a very select few restaurants in the industry specializing specifically in chicken wings, Wild Wing differentiates itself from competitors offering a more traditional product. Further driving Wild Wing's differentiation is the extremely customizable nature of their focused product offering. While most restaurants serve between three and six chicken wing flavours, Wild Wing offers upwards of one hundred wing flavours, the largest flavour offering in the Ontario restaurant industry. Unusual flavours like "Smoked Chocolate" and "Dill Pickle" give Wild Wing customers something they cannot get anywhere else.

2 Strong Franchising System

To grow from a small-town, one-man operation to over sixty restaurants across the province in about ten years, Wild Wing had to develop a strong franchising system. The first key aspect of this system is that they demand lower franchise fees than the average restaurant, which makes investment in a Wild Wing franchise significantly more attractive to potential franchisees.

Second, Wild Wing has an effective plan in place for locating and establishing franchises. The corporate office operates as a "restaurant supply group," handling the construction of buildings. Each franchisee obtains the right to use the Wild Wing Restaurants name, trademark, image, logo, and procedures through the term of the franchise agreement (ten years). Franchise management follows the company's concept, to ensure consistency throughout the Wild Wing chain. The company also provides continuous support in all areas of the business to each franchisee under the terms of the franchise agreement.

3 Friendly Restaurant Atmosphere

A key component of a restaurant's success is the atmosphere and feeling one gets in the restaurant. Wild Wing does an excellent job of creating a comfortable atmosphere that appeals to many people. The lights are bright and the space is relatively open, unlike many modern restaurants that aim to provide a mysterious, private atmosphere. Wild Wing's atmosphere is social and lively, with country music playing and TVs broadcasting sports around the restaurant. Wild Wing restaurants are relatively small as well, giving an impression of being busy and crowded, further enhancing the social atmosphere. This image also fits in well with the major target market – large groups. Groups want to eat at a place that isn't overly formal, and where socialization and interaction are encouraged, not limited.

Strategic Opportunities

While Wild Wing has already made great strides through their expansion across Ontario, there are still opportunities that exist to become an even more significant player in the restaurant industry.

1 Further Expansion

At this point, Wild Wing has over sixty locations either operating or soon to be operating across Ontario. While there may still be some opportunities that exist in Ontario, the real opportunity for Wild Wing at this point lies outside of the province. Expansion into Quebec or the Prairie Provinces is certainly viable, and both Western and Atlantic Canada may not be far-off targets. Wild Wing has stated that their goal is to expand beyond Ontario, and, by making initial forays into Quebec, Manitoba, or Saskatchewan, Wild Wing could take a major step towards realizing this goal.

2 Aggressive Targeting of Teams and Groups

The atmosphere at Wild Wing is particularly conducive to large groups, as is the product offering. It is an especially attractive location for sports teams who often go out to eat and drink following games. Because of the natural appeal that Wild Wing holds to sports teams, it makes sense for them to aggressively target these groups through promotions and special discounts in an effort to become the premier post-game team hangout in Ontario.

---

time, idea sharing and networking opportunities for entrepreneurs are available. For more information on business incubation and a listing of the business incubators in Canada, visit the Canadian Association of Business Incubation's website, http://www.cabi.ca.

PROVIDE VALUABLE INFORMATION

At all stages of the business development cycle, entrepreneurs need to have appropriate, up-to-date information, e.g., regarding resources and markets as such, community leaders can be of great assistance by helping to find relevant business information and publishing it on community websites. Such information can be categorized in the following ways.[39]

Information about Financial Resources

To choose appropriate sources of financing, entrepreneurs need to be aware of the spectrum of financial resources available both in and outside their community. Entrepreneurs can be made aware of business lending programs, government programs, and online resources. Additional information on financing options is provided in Chapter 11.

Information about Professional Services

Entrepreneurs often need to use services provided by professionals such as accountants, lawyers, and business consultants. Community leaders can contact the chamber of commerce or existing businesses in the local area to learn more about the available professional services. They can make this information widely known (e.g., via a community website).

Information about Physical Infrastructure

Community leaders can take inventory of available buildings that entrepreneurs can use to set up their businesses. The available spaces and their approximate rents or purchase prices should be listed as well.

Information about Markets

Community leaders can conduct surveys to find out which goods and services residents shop for outside the community. Potential entrepreneurs can use this information to better assess whether there is an adequate market for a new business. Community leaders can also take an inventory of existing businesses. This can help entrepreneurs determine the level of competition that exists in a particular market.

Information about Tax Strategies for Small Businesses

Entrepreneurs must effectively manage their business revenue and expenses. Web-based resources such as http://www.sbinfocanada. about.com/cs/taxinfo/a/taxstrategies.htm offer simple yet effective and practical strategies.

DEVELOPING THE SKILLS OF ENTREPRENEURS

Some believe that entrepreneurs are born possessing a certain set of traits. However, others argue that entrepreneurs are made; in other words, entrepreneurship involves a set of skills that is the result of development rather than innate endowment.[40] Accordingly, communities should concentrate their efforts on developing skills that will allow entrepreneurs to succeed. Skill development can be of great benefit to entrepreneurs at various stages of the business life cycle.

Two prominent academics studying entrepreneurship, Thomas Lyons and Gregg Lichtenstein, have developed a system of enterprise development that focuses on the concept of developing entrepreneurs. This approach is called the Entrepreneurial Development System (EDS) and has been implemented and shown to be effective in several communities in the United States. It is built on three major premises: (1) Ultimate success in entrepreneurship requires the mastery of a set of skills, (2) these skills can be developed, and, (3) entrepreneurs do not all come to entrepreneurship with the same skill level.[41]

According to Lyons, skills that are relevant to successful entrepreneurship can be classified into four major categories:

- Technical Skills – needed to engage in the entrepreneur's industry
- Managerial Skills – needed for day-to-day business activities
- Entrepreneurial Skills – having the ability to act on market opportunities and come up with innovative solutions to business challenges
- Personal Maturity Skills – self-awareness, accountability, emotional coping, and creativity skills

The Entrepreneurial Development System is a program that involves various community professionals who take on specific roles and perform functions related to skill assessment and development.

- The *Scout* identifies and recruits potential entrepreneurs and assesses their commitment to entrepreneurship.
- The *Diagnostician* assesses the entrepreneurs' needs and skill levels and ascertains the obstacles they face to get the resources they require for success. The diagnostician also has an in-depth knowledge of the range of services available in the community. Thus, the diagnostician can refer entrepreneurs to appropriate service providers. The assessments made by the scout and the diagnostician allow for a "game plan" to be formed for an entrepreneur. This plan is highly customized and is based on the current skill set of the entrepreneur and how far along his or her business is in the business life cycle.
- The *Performance Coach* provides one-on-one guidance and mentorship to individual entrepreneurs who want to develop their

skills and improve their performance. Coaches are often individuals with entrepreneurial experience who have achieved business success. They actively develop entrepreneurs' thinking and ability to adapt to changing circumstances. They also help entrepreneurs develop personal maturity skills.

• The *Success Team Manager* coordinates a group of entrepreneurs who operate at the same level of development or in the same market or industry. He or she facilitates the sharing of information and resources to deal with common business issues. This allows entrepreneurs to develop their skills together and learn from each other.

It is critical to note that rural communities may not have the resources to hire all these professionals to take on these roles. However, community leaders can learn from the EDS and apply some of its ideas. They can delegate individuals to perform a subset of these functions. For instance, individuals who work in business incubators may be able to play some of these roles.

CREATE NETWORKING OPPORTUNITIES

An entrepreneurial community fosters networks for entrepreneurs to learn from each other.[42] Horizontal networks (e.g., a network of entrepreneurs) are beneficial because entrepreneurs can give and receive guidance and feedback. Such networks help to create a learning community; such a community enables its members to obtain new knowledge, share insights with other members, and modify behaviour to reflect what has been learned.[43] These networks also allow for entrepreneurs to collaborate and collectively accomplish goals. Cooperation, not competition, is more likely to foster rural economic activity.[44]

Community leaders can promote networking in a number of ways. First, they can encourage their local chamber of commerce to organize social events and business meetings.[45] On a larger scale, leaders can establish an independent organization or association of entrepreneurs in a community. Calgary, for example, has a formal networking group of entrepreneurs, The Calgary Entrepreneur Meet-up Group that hosts social events and speaker series.[46] Membership in this networking group is free and open to all business owners. In addition, as mentioned earlier, community leaders can

Building Community and Business Networks – Silver Connections

http://www.silverconnections.ca

Silver Connections is a community referral service that was created in Brock Township and the City of Kawartha Lakes. The partners, Twila Del Fatti and Barb Smith, incorporated in November 2007 and rolled out their concept in March 2008. The company screens other businesses and then refers them to consumers who want reassurance that they are dealing with reputable firms. The businesses that join the Silver Connections network fund the program by paying a nominal annual fee, but the service is free to those in the community who use it (e.g., new residents, seniors, people with disabilities, community non-profit agencies, busy professionals, and new businesses).

The partners refer to their business as a "three-pronged plug." They help consumers find businesses that offer them sterling customer service and perform the required tasks. They also help build small businesses through driving business to them as well as by giving feedback on customer experiences. Finally, they are "grounded" by their connections to the non-profit agencies and organizations in their communities that offer so much with little or no charge to their clients.

Silver Connections staff believes that connecting with non-profit as well as for-profit organizations should be an integral part of any business plan. They attend Chamber of Commerce meetings in all the communities that they serve and seek out other networking groups whose members share their perspective on the importance of connections. They also think that sharing information with others is a good way to collectively address issues that businesses struggle with and ultimately enhance everyone's opportunity for success.

One example of their networking efforts is the founding of the Brock Networking Group. Brock Township, the most northern part of Durham Region, is home to three small villages: Beaverton, Cannington, and Sunderland. Twila and Barb initiated the networking group as a way to link the business communities within the three urban centres and ultimately strengthen the whole municipality by encouraging the businesses to support each other.

The Brock Networking group meets monthly, offering a breakfast meeting session to accommodate business owners' schedules. There are no membership fees or a formal organization structure – a simple RSVP is the only requirement. At each meeting, business owners are invited to introduce themselves and their businesses so that other attendees can get to know them and the services they provide. One business is invited to be the "Feature" business and the owner is allotted ten minutes for additional marketing of products or services.

"We have found that these meetings help us know our neighbours so that we can put a face to the name and in a small community, that is important." Twila Del Fatti

"When relationships are made, the community becomes stronger. It is important to build the element of trust before referring businesses to neighbours and friends." Barb Smith

encourage the development of business incubators; incubators naturally allow for networking opportunities since all businesses operate under one roof making collaboration more likely.

SUMMARY

The creative economy offers significant opportunities for rural communities to rebuild their vitality. However, it is critical to understand its principles. Examining the strategies of communities that are leaders in embracing this new economy provides valuable instruction for rural communities who want to test new approaches. It is important to note that successful approaches in one community will not necessarily work elsewhere. Building on community assets and local knowledge is the key.

CED practitioners can use a variety of techniques to encourage entrepreneurship including offering opportunities for entrepreneurs to build their skills and access financing. Community leaders can support an entrepreneurial climate formally by creating business incubators and informally by promoting networking among local businesses.

7

New Economic Opportunities from Skilled Trades and Value-added Thinking

While the creative economy offers rural communities opportunities for economic diversification and revitalization, there are yet many new economic opportunities to be found in traditional industries, including manufacturing, trades, agriculture, and forestry. In many of these sectors, however, skilled labour is becoming increasingly scarce. To harness the economic potential of these industries, then, rural communities must encourage skilled trades in the labour force. Likewise, it is crucial for traditional industries to adopt an entrepreneurial spirit to find new opportunities for profitability and growth in a changing, and increasingly global, marketplace. In this context, it is crucial for firms to develop innovative, value-added offerings from traditional natural resources to succeed in the new economy.

The economic sustainability of rural communities is heavily dependent on their ability to attract and retain skilled and experienced tradespeople. While skilled workers tend to enjoy a significant (e.g., 40 per cent) wage premium over unskilled workers, the latter are also more likely to be unemployed or underemployed and tend to require more social assistance. Despite this, most rural areas in Ontario are currently experiencing chronic shortages of skilled tradespeople. Projections suggest that such shortages will increase in the future due to the following:

- Overall shortages of skilled trades workers – For instance, it is estimated that Ontario will experience a shortage of approximately 100,000 skilled trades workers in the manufacturing sector alone over the next fifteen or so years.

- Growing presence of older workers in the labour market – Projections indicate that the number of retirees will exceed the number of new entrants by 2016.
- Negative public perception of the trades – Many young people and their parents view the skilled trades as a last resort option.
- Lack of visibility and promotion – In one survey, 72 per cent of young people said their guidance counselors did not encourage skilled trades as a career option, while another survey found that 37 per cent of young people said their schools did not have accessible information on skilled trades.
- Relatively low apprenticeship rates – Recent research suggests that only 18 per cent of employers utilize apprentices, largely because they tend to see such programs as costly.

Municipal leaders in partnership with the education system and the community can utilize a number of strategies to ensure that opportunities for skilled trades professionals are maximized. These strategies can include:

- Developing a sound understanding of the region's specific skilled trades needs:
  - Conduct local research on the supply and demand in the trades to gain an understanding of the local needs and opportunities.
  - Initiate and participate in round tables, discussion forums, and conferences on trades-related issues at the local level.
  - Evaluate the apprenticeship completion rates in the local area.
- Working towards enhancing the image and status of skilled trades:
  - Initiate activities to build awareness of trades at an early age (e.g., at elementary school levels) by using innovative promotional materials and campaigns that appeal to youth.
  - Create a Rural Trade & Skills Teacher of the Year Award to encourage teachers to play active roles in trades' promotion.
  - Bring together employers, government officials, and dignitaries that have success stories related to the enhancement of skilled trades.
  - Organize a summer trades camp that provides opportunities for young people to find out about different trades and initiate skills development.
- Developing visible avenues of entrance into skilled trades:

- Generate and distribute a comprehensive list of trades schools and programs in the immediate and surrounding areas.
- Build awareness of and engagement in trades by hosting local trades fairs.
- Arrange for employers and other stakeholders to speak at local schools, businesses, conferences, and community events.
- Create newsletters that contain trades information relevant to local community members.

• Creating partnerships and networks that allow for coordination and communication between key stakeholders (students, parents, teachers, employers, government agencies, community groups, etc.):

- Develop a central website that contains trades resources and information, and allows local employers to post job opportunities and job seekers to post resumes.
- Support local businesses in the development of promotional materials describing the company's work, types of careers offered, and expectations of workers. This support can include arranging school visits and company tours.
- Support the development and maintenance of local mentorship and apprenticeship programs. Provide or identify financial incentives that help alleviate the burden on employers of developing and maintaining these programs. Develop a *clearing house* that keeps employers informed about related incentives and activities.

GOVERNMENT-FUNDED PROGRAMS

A number of government-funded programs directly promote the development of skilled trades by providing support and opportunities to students, employers and educational institutions. Details of sample programs are provided in Appendix E.

Rural communities can also benefit from partnering with Local Boards (e.g., the Local Boards of Ontario). These are not-for-profit, community-based organizations composed of volunteers from business, labour, education, and community groups. Their mandate is to work at the local level to develop solutions to labour market needs and issues that have been identified. They do this by engaging community stakeholders and partners in labour market research and planning that leverages cooperative efforts. More information can be found at http://www.localboards.on.ca.

Skills Development Success Stories
Lanark and Renfrew Counties in collaboration with St.
Lawrence College
In 2007, in response to skill shortages, an unskilled workforce, and a reluctance of employers to take on apprentices, Lanark and Renfrew Counties in collaboration with St. Lawrence College created an apprenticeship brochure titled "Making Cent$ of Apprenticeship." The brochure contained information about the benefits of apprenticeship to both prospective employers and apprentices. Another successful endeavour was a Skilled Trades Fair aimed at providing information and guidance to youth regarding work in skilled trades. The fair was attended by 1,540 people and featured sixty-two exhibits from thirty-six organizations. A Rural Road Show was also launched in 2007 that provided the residents of Middleville and Lanark with information about the training and job opportunities in their areas. Eighteen service providers participated and over fifty individuals attended. Other planned actions to address skilled trades issues in Renfrew and Lanark Counties included the development of a fact sheet on the benefits to employers of taking on apprentices, implementation of a survey to determine skills shortages in local labour markets, and active encouragement of employers with skill shortages to sit on a "Champions Committee" aimed at addressing employer reluctance to take on apprentices. For more information, visit http://www.algonquincollege.com/renfrewlanarkworkforce/Apprenticeship.htm.

SLOME (Skills London Oxford Middlesex Elgin)
Another successful trades initiative was developed by the Elgin, Middlesex, Oxford Local Training Board in Western Ontario. SLOME (Skills London Oxford Middlesex Elgin), an independent not-for-profit project, is an annual hands-on skills competition and career exploration day designed to provide over 4,300 local students with interactive information and opportunities about skilled trades. This initiative links the private, public, and educational communities in developing positive publicity about skilled trades. In 2007, more than sixty-five local organizations and private businesses displayed exhibits at the event. The final SLOME event was held in May 2012 after reaching more than 27,000 students.

GEORGINA TRADES TRAINING, INC.

Communities in the South Lake CFDC region improved the local trades school through an innovative program at Georgina Trades Training, Inc. (GTTI). GTTI is a community-based learning centre in the Lake Simcoe area. It is the result of a unique partnership among public and private secondary school boards and municipal, provincial and federal government organizations to provide trades training. Courses and training are provided through educational partners, and are offered in both on-line and on-site modules. Further information is available online at http://www.gtti.ca.

CREATING VALUE-ADDED OFFERINGS

In addition to developing labour skills, it is critical that firms operating in traditional industries, especially natural resource-based sectors, develop creative product and service offerings. Ontario's agriculture and forestry sectors are developing value-added products from local natural resources. At the most basic level, added value can come from either transforming a product in some way, or providing an additional service which complements the product itself. Specific solutions vary from resource to resource and are dependent on many factors including resource availability, location, skills, and knowledge base. However, the following examples offer ideas that may be helpful to other communities.

Adding Value through Experiences

Milton is located in Southern Ontario, about 40 km west of Toronto. It made headlines when the results of the 2006 census named the town the fastest-growing community in Canada. The population at the last census stood at 53,900 residents, an increase of 71.4 per cent over the previous five years.[1] However, this community is rooted in an agricultural past and is still surrounded by many active farms. Established in 1957 in Milton, Ontario, Chudleigh's (http://www. chudleighs.com) has evolved from a "pick-your-own" orchard to a thriving business encompassing both an entertainment farm and a commercial bakery. The orchard has an on-site children's play area, restaurant and retail store which sells baked goods, crafts and other related products. Nearby, the commercial bakery provides goods for a number of grocery stores across North America. Chudleigh's

Fast Facts
Fifth Town Artisan Cheese
http://www.fifthtown.ca

Location: East of Picton, Prince Edward County, Ontario

Key Products: Artisan sheep and goat cheese

Success Factors:
- High quality
- Green sustainability model
- Strategic partnerships
- Differentiated business strategy

Case Study – Fifth Town Artisan Cheese

Company Overview and Background

Fifth Town Artisan Cheese Company is an environmentally and socially responsible rural business competing in the artisan cheese category. Located east of Picton in Prince Edward County, Fifth Town is positioned as a niche producer of sixteen quality, handmade cheeses made using locally produced goat and sheep milk. Since opening in July 2008, Fifth Town has achieved sales of $1.3 million and in 2009 became one of the first Canadian companies to be accredited under the Leadership in Energy and Environmental Design (LEED) program. Fifth Town products appear in gourmet grocery stores in Toronto and Ottawa, high-end restaurants and hotel chains, as well as at partner retail outlets at wineries and cheese companies throughout Prince Edward County. Its high quality products justify a higher price. In this way, Fifth Town is able to generate profits from its sale of artisan cheeses and complementary products.

Industry Overview

The cheese industry is broken down into industrial cheeses and artisan cheeses. In Canada, the industrial cheese category is dominated by Saputo Inc., Kraft Canada Inc., Agropur Cooperative Ltd., and Parmalat Canada Ltd. These companies mass produce industrial cheese products and distribute them using multinational grocery chains. The industrial cheese category is growing at 1–3 per cent annually.

The artisan specialty cheese industry is composed of 200 different producers across Canada, with the majority based in Quebec. In the past few years, demand for artisan specialty cheeses using locally produced, organic ingredients has been on the rise achieving a growth rate of approximately 20 per cent.

Key Success Factors

Three factors have been identified as key drivers for Fifth Town's success and competitive advantage:

1 High Quality

Fifth Town has ingrained quality throughout its entire organization in its products, people, processes, and plant. Fifth Town only purchases raw milk inputs from local Prince Edward County farmers, in order for its cheeses to truly take on the unique taste of the land in that region. Three certified cheesemakers within the seven-person operation bring excellence and expertise to the cheese-making process. The safety and cleanliness standards required for raw milk producing factories are met through additional investments that achieve the highest quality and most sanitary production methods. The equipment and state of the art facility was designed by an experienced team of engineers and architects collaborating to create a sustainable operation.

2 Green Sustainability Model

Fifth Town's commitment to a green business model builds customer loyalty and allows for future operational cost savings. The facility achieved Platinum LEED accreditation in March 2009. A bio-digestive waste system sits behind the facilities, where byproducts are converted into biomass. Fifth Town also pays a premium for biodegradable packaging that encourages consumers to compost leftover materials. The company strives to operate with little to no waste.

Eighty per cent of Fifth Town's building is made of recycled materials. An on-site windmill and built-in solar panels provide renewable energy. Also, forty miles of geothermal pipeline is installed horizontally underground. The natural cheese-aging cave is regulated by the geothermal system rather than by traditional, energy-intensive refrigeration units. Fifth Town is also included in Bullfrog Power's carbon-free electricity network, paying a premium for its additional energy requirements. The uniquely designed facility operates at 30 per cent energy levels of the baseline construction requirements.

3 Strategic Partnerships

Another essential building block of Fifth Town's success is its ability to lever strategic partnerships. Working together with suppliers, other local cheese producers, wineries, and government organizations enables Fifth Town to capitalize on cost reductions, marketing synergies, and expansion opportunities.

Cooper worked directly with Fifth Town's six suppliers to convert to Local Food Plus standards. Local Food Plus is the Ontario standard for sustainable food, which is at the forefront of changing consumer preferences towards sustainable, local agriculture. Co-marketing with wineries also contributes to higher sales and increased perceived product quality.

Lessons Learned

Fifth Town capitalized on its core competencies to drive success through the implementation of five key strategies in relation to planning, development, management, and operational aspects of the business. These approaches may assist other small and mid-sized rural businesses.

First, business owners can examine their management team. Ideally, this group will be committed to, and have a strong passion for, the business. Second, businesses can identify a niche product and/or develop a theme. Fifth Town has developed a theme bound by its commitment towards being "green." Everything from the inputs, to the manufacturing process and final product encompasses the green theme. Not only does this give Fifth Town a unique product, but it also provides it with significant access to specific target markets.

Third, business owners can leverage advantages offered to them by their surroundings. Fifth Town's entire business model is aligned with the Prince Edward County Region's focus on local resources. Fourth, firms can build strong partnerships. For Fifth Town, the strong partnerships that it has built with its suppliers as well as local food organizations have made doing business easier. Finally, businesses can take advantage of a range of financing opportunities that are available; Fifth Town did.

In summary, Fifth Town Artisan Cheese Company has developed a competitive niche in the artisan specialty cheese category. Their approach to business means "preserving the environment while striving to delight and surprise the discerning palate." This simple motto captures the essence of Fifth Town's differentiated business strategy, and its significant success.

---

provides a good case study for examining how to add value to raw resources.

As with many farms in Ontario, Chudleigh's originally adopted a pick-your-own business model because it reduced overhead costs by transferring labour to customers. This approach was appealing to customers who would come out, pick a large amount of fruits and

Case Study – The Green Beaver Company

Company Overview and Background

Green Beaver was founded in Hawkesbury in 2003 by Alain Menard and Karen Clark, with the goal of creating healthy, natural products without the use of chemicals. Their product line includes shampoos, conditioners, body washes, and lotions, whose ingredients are natural, vegan, and gluten-free, and 95 per cent of which are or ganically grown or ecologically wild-crafted in Canada. Green Beaver is a member of the Canadian Health Foods Association (CHFA), an organic trade association started in 2008.

Fast Facts
The Green Beaver Company
http://www.greenbeaver.com
Location: Hawkesbury, Prescott-Russell, Ontario
Key Products: Green product line including hair and body cleansers and lotions
Success Factors:
- Unique strategic mission
- Reputation
- Product differentiation
- Customer relationships
- Retailer relationships

In 2008, Green Beaver purchased 10,000 square feet of production space for the purposes of margin control, quality control, and lead-time control. This included a laboratory to develop samples; inventory space to hold raw materials and finished products; a batch room used to mix products; and a filling room which packages each bottle, labels products, and packs them into boxes.

Green Beaver's main target customers are new mothers who are concerned about the possible harmful effects of chemicals on their babies and who shop at natural health food stores. Currently 3,000 retail locations across Canada carry the Green Beaver brand. Green Beaver estimates that they own approximately 2 per cent of the organic natural health products market.

Industry Overview

The organic natural health products market originated in France, spread quickly throughout the European Union, and is now growing in North America. With research shedding more light on the disadvantages of chemical ingredients, the awareness of and desire for organic products have increased. As such, the market growth for organic natural health products in recent years has been between 15 and 20 per cent.

In order to truly distinguish organic natural health products in the market, ECOCERT is a private company in France that audits and provides accreditation to organic producers. They conduct one scheduled audit and one unscheduled audit each year to check the ingredients going into each participating manufacturer's products. Currently, 25 per cent of the natural health products market demands ECOCERT, but this demand is expected to grow. There are only two ECOCERT-certified organic producers in Canada, one of which is Green Beaver.

Organic natural health products are usually sold in specialty health food stores. However, because of the small number of distribution outlets in Canada, Green Beaver is concerned about the limited opportunities for growth in the country, and therefore believes that penetrating the United States market would promote more long-term sustainable growth for the company.

Key Success Factors

1 Unique strategic mission
Green Beaver focuses their efforts on providing 100 per cent organic products to differentiate themselves from other companies in the industry. Meanwhile, Green Beaver is determined to remain a small and personal company that distributes products primarily to specialty health food stores and avoids large chains to maintain a strong consumer shopping experience. Consumer education is also at the forefront of their operations, providing them with another reason to distribute their products through specialty stores.

2 Reputation
Green Beaver is a member of the Canadian Health Foods Association and one of the two Canadian companies certified by ECOCERT. Although this certification is not yet widely recognized in North America, it is likely to provide Green Beaver with a competitive advantage in the future. The company predicts that eventually new regulations for the cosmetics industry will be established given current trends in Europe. They already comply with these regulations and will thus have an advantage.

3 Product Differentiation
Green Beaver products are effective and safe for customers and the environment. As described earlier, their ingredients and methods are 100 per cent organic, which makes them unique in the industry, as most of the other personal care products in the market labeled as "organic" contain up to 5 per cent synthetic ingredients. Their products are also competitive in terms of

price, being the cheapest in the 100 per cent organic cosmetics segment in Canada.

4 Customer relationships

Green Beaver establishes strong relationships with their customers by providing them with natural and safe products, which also prove to be as effective as the synthetic ones. The company has built a base of loyal customers, who use their products repeatedly. Customer loyalty is significant. The company primarily relies on favourable word of mouth reports to market the brand.

5 Retailer relationships

The small size of the company is beneficial for creating and strengthening relationships with retailers. It allows Green Beaver to respond quickly and flexibly to the demand for their products. By maintaining direct and close contact with retailers, Green Beaver gets favourable terms, such as better shelf placement, not to mention store employees who promote the products.

Lessons Learned

It is evident that Green Beaver is succeeding within the organic natural health products industry by leveraging core competencies, a unique company strategy, great corporate reputation, high quality products, and favourable customer and retailer relationships. There is significant growth potential present within this specialized industry, and Green Beaver is well positioned to grow.

---

vegetables, and then return home to make preserves to last throughout the winter. Recently, however, several societal changes reduced the profitability of this model.

First, there was an increase in the number of families where both adults worked full-time. Second, the advent of Sunday shopping created greater competition from retail stores. Both of these factors resulted in people having less free time and more activities competing for that time. Furthermore, globalization and improved transportation systems enabled grocery stores to bring in fresh fruit year-round at reasonable costs. In addition, the art of making preserves gradually disappeared with each new generation, as the need

Case Study – Pefferlaw Peat Products

Company Overview and Background

Pefferlaw Peat Products (PPP) opened its doors in 1954, when G.T. Strain and his sons began harvesting soil from their bog in Pefferlaw, Ontario. It was incorporated in 1977 and then sold to its current owner, Peter Prust. Mr. Prust saw an immediate opportunity to improve the operation by investing in new equipment, which he purchased and put into use within three months of acquiring the company.

Today, the company harvests, manufactures, and packages soil products intended for home gardening. Raw materials are sourced from their "backyard" bog as well as from external suppliers. PPP produces a wide product line using various ratios of inputs such as peat humus, peat fibre, and manures. PPP focuses on business-to-business sales, and although they sell to large retailers such as Canadian Tire, their main customers are independent garden centres within a three-hour drive from their site.

Market Segmentation

At the product level, it is difficult to create a differentiated soil. Technically speaking, all soils serve the same purpose at almost equal effectiveness, and, as such, segmentation in this market is due to perceived differences more than anything else. In the soil market, products have been divided largely into entry level and premium soils. Although this division exists, there is little difference between the two product segments. This makes packaging and marketing of even greater importance in order to establish strong brand recognition.

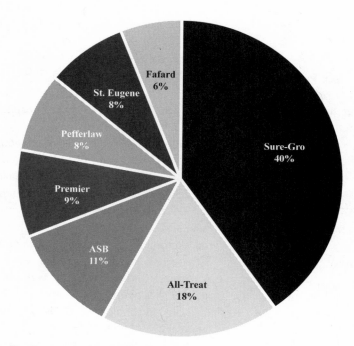

Figure D – Percent Market Share of Ontario Soil Supply

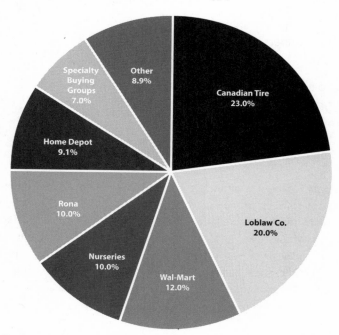

Figure E – Percent of Total Ontario Soil Production Bought by Retailer (by Store)

Industry and Competitors

PPP faces strong competition from a number of local producers. As a result of the 2008 acquisition of Modugno-Hortibec, Sure-Gro became the Canadian leader, controlling 40 per cent of the market (see Figure D). It is important to note that the figures exclude a large player within the industry: Scotts Miracle Gro, a $3 billion, publicly-traded, global giant. Unlike the companies listed in Exhibit A, Scotts is in a position to invest in extensive research and development, and more importantly, marketing.

All these firms operate in a business-to-business environment, selling their products to garden centres of various stores. Distribution through Canadian Tire and the various banners of Loblaw Companies drives a higher volume (see Figure E). The nature of the product is such that it does not go through distribution intermediaries and it cannot be shipped far from the production facility because the bags are large, heavy, and prone to breaking. Also, margins are relatively low and shipping is a major expense. An interesting point of differentiation, however, is that PPP's products are certified organic, although to date this has not significantly increased sales.

It appears that the industry is saturated and stagnating. Even Scotts, after spending nearly $300 million in advertising through 2007 and 2008, only grew year-over-year sales by 2 per cent. A key way to increase sales is by gaining market share, which, with an undifferentiated, similarly priced product, is a difficult task.

Key Success Factors

1 Product Quality and Brand Loyalty
Soil customers primarily care about the results that a particular brand of soil yields. If the product they purchase provides satisfactory results on the first attempt, often they will be loyal to that particular brand regardless of other factors that come into play. Their satisfaction and loyalty can potentially boost demand via word-of-mouth advertising. Conversely, poor results discourage customers and create a negative bias toward the brand that is difficult to overcome.

2 Packaging
Since the various brands of soil exhibit few differentiating factors at the product characteristics level, it can be difficult for consumers to make a purchasing decision. Consumers rely on the suggestions of staff or may purchase the product with the most appealing packaging. PPP has two types of

packages: brightly-coloured bags with pictures of flowers for the premium products, and plain-coloured bags for entry-level products. The different kinds of fertilizers are colour-coded for easier repeat purchases. This feature has been a success in the marketplace.

3 Pricing
The price range for soil and fertilizer products is between $2.99 and $6.99 for a typical 30 L bag. The price floor is based on consumers' perceptions; anything priced lower is considered to be of poor quality. The price ceiling has been established over time by the market; pricing above the ceiling results in poor sales because well-known, trusted brands are sold for less. PPP's product line covers the entire price range.

4 Lean Manufacturing
Pefferlaw Peat Products runs a very lean operation, allowing it to maintain low levels of overhead. It has very few employees, both in administrative and operational functions, and no unnecessary office space. Cost-consciousness runs throughout the business, and every decision is evaluated on how it impacts the overall cost structure.

Future Opportunities

PPP could further differentiate its products, grow brand loyalty, and drive sales to higher levels through enhanced marketing efforts. The lack of a dedicated sales team makes it difficult for the company to expand its customer base and market reach, and subsequently to increase sales.

Another option to consider would be that of forming a bargaining unit with other producers in the Ontario market. Under a single brand name and promotional campaign, their products could gain wider brand recognition in a highly undifferentiated market, helping to increase negotiation power with retail purchasers and brand loyalty with customers. These pooled resources would help spread out and streamline marketing and promotional costs. By establishing this bargaining unit, PPP would be able to expand its market reach and market share, and therefore enjoy increased sales and revenue growth.

and the time available were both on the decline. The net result of these factors was that people who showed up to pick-your-own farms were fewer in number and were purchasing fewer fruits and vegetables.

One grower in the Toronto area calculated that in the early 1990s, the average per-person sale was $8, and each person ate $1 worth of fruit while picking (a self-administered discount which was seen as fair by both parties). By the early 2000s, this had switched to an average purchase of $0.80 and an eating discount of $1.50.[2] Clearly, this model was no longer feasible for growers. What emerged, though, was a new model that seems to be working.

Research in marketing has long recognized that when people buy a product, they are really purchasing a service. In other words, people buy products to help achieve a goal that they have. For example, a person will buy a drill not to own the product, but rather because of the tasks it allows him or her to complete (e.g., to make holes). This service-oriented view of consumption is closely related to an experiential view of purchases, where people pursue options that involve "fantasies, feelings, and fun."[3] Recently, the ideas of co-creation and co-production have become important in marketing research, as companies try to find new and better ways to attract and keep customers.[4] The premise of co-creation and co-production is that people will see value in being able to immerse themselves in the consumption process as active participants.

In the case of farms such as Chudleigh's, the owners are realizing that people are no longer coming out of necessity, but rather for the experience of being on a working farm. Given that more children are growing up with only a rough idea about where their food comes from, going to a farm has become a family outing. Out of the ashes of the pick-your-own model, the entertainment farm has emerged.

Also known as agritourism, the entertainment farm can require a change in perspective for many farm owners. In addition to all of the work involved in raising livestock and/or growing crops, this model requires that owners also take on the role of show person, mixing with the public and providing staff to take care of customer needs. Creating an entertainment farm also requires the construction of attractions that will bring customers to the location. These can include mazes (rope or corn), zoos, pony rides, play structures, and on-site restaurants. One study found that people are looking for an

Agriculture Entertainment Enterprises

Wineries with Friday happy hours
Arts & crafts demonstrations
Farm stores
Roadside stands
Processing demonstrations
Cider pressing
Antique villages
Herb walks
Workshops
Festivals
Cooking demos
Pick-your-own
Pumpkin patches
Rent-an-apple-tree
Moonlight activities
Pageants
Speakers
Regional themes
Mazes
Crop art
Pancake breakfasts during sugaring season
Bad weather accommodations
Tastings
Buffalo
Dude ranches
Educational tours
Farm schools
K–12 schools
Outdoor schools
Challenge schools
Movement-based retreat centres
Native American villages
Frontier villages
Collections of old farm machinery
Miniature villages
Farm theme playgrounds for children
Fantasylands
Gift shops
Antiques
Crafts
Crafts demonstrations
Food sales
Lunch counters
Cold drinks
Restaurants
Pizza farms
Native prairies preservation
August "Dog Days" – 50% off dogwoods if customer brings picture of family dog, etc.
Campgrounds
Indian mounds, earthworks art
Historical re-creations
Living history farms
Heirloom plants and animals
Historic agricultural structures
Log buildings
Maple sugaring
Sheep shearing
Wool processing
Grain milling
Apple butter making
Fee fishing/ hunting
Farm vacations
Bed and breakfasts
Farm tours
Horseback riding
Cross-country skiing
Camping
Hay rides
Sleigh rides
Rest areas for snowmobilers or cross-country skiers
Themes (apple town, etc.)
Picnic grounds
Shady spots for travelers to rest
Hieroglyphics, rock art
Hunting lodges

average of four hours of entertainment for each hour they need to drive, so the entertainment needs to satisfy this demand.[5]

The entertainment farm can also be an opportunity to showcase local talents in a centralized location. It can contain a gift shop with crafts and small gifts available for purchase. In a symbiotic relationship, the gift shop can seek out local artists and craftspeople to display their work in person, benefitting both parties.

In addition to directly serving families and other customers, farm owners can use the facilities of an entertainment farm to provide educational tours. For example, the Ontario Ministry of Education curriculum requires students to be taught the differences between urban and rural life, and also includes food units that highlight farming.[6] Country Heritage Park, another facility in Milton, offers an interactive educational experience that takes advantage of the region's farming history. This museum-like site has collected a variety of exhibits and artifacts and displays them in a natural setting, with costumed staff to "showcase the evolution of rural life and food production in Ontario."[7] Chudleigh's also offers programs for local schools in the fall where they teach fruit growing and processing to students.

Examples of entertainment farms already exist in Eastern Ontario, and showcase opportunities for adding value to a working farm. In the town of Munster, just outside of Ottawa, the Saunders Farm offers seasonal entertainment such as a maze and spray park, and special Halloween-themed attractions. The farm also promotes itself as a location for special events such as weddings and corporate retreats.[8] Similarly, the McMaze farm, located in St. Andrews West, just north of Cornwall, offers year-round entertainment opportunities.[9] A unique offering at McMaze is the pumpkin seed planting opportunity in the spring. Visitors are encouraged to plant a pumpkin seed and return frequently to watch it grow – an innovative way to promote repeat visits.

The Haliburton Forest and Wild Life Reserve demonstrates that experiential attractions need not be limited to crop growing farms.[10] This organization has taken advantage of available natural resources and built attractions that *highlight* the unique features of the area, with canopy tours taking people through the treetops and educational programs. The Wilton Cheese Factory in Odessa is another example of a facility that offers experiential entertainment (e.g., a wedding location and tours), but also demonstrates another option for adding value to resources – by processing them and selling the finished goods.[11]

Adding Value through Production

Although entertainment farming may work for communities located near population centres, this may not be an option in more remote locations. In this case, another option for adding value to raw resources is required, and one where Chudleigh's again provides a possible solution. In addition to the entertainment farm business, Chudleigh's has also developed a commercial production facility.

Chudleigh's bakery began as a small-scale operation serving the local community (and the on-site restaurant) with fresh baked goods. In 1990, a fire started in a remote building and spread to destroy the retail store, bakery, and cider press. Despite this setback, the business continued to grow, and now the current commercial facility, rebuilt in 2007, is an 82,000 ft² bakery employing 150 full-time staff. The Apple Blossoms (Chudleigh's signature dessert), pies and other desserts are now available through a number of locations, including Metro and M&M Meat Shops. By integrating the processing of the raw resources, the owners saw an opportunity to add value by using available skills and resources and focusing on a few key products.

Current marketing research suggests that organizations add value to products by embedding them with knowledge and skills. Along each step in the process, from raw resources to finished product, someone makes a contribution by changing the product and passing it along. For example, the farmer has knowledge about the soil and water tables on his or her land and the required skills to produce the crop of wheat. The wheat gets transported to a mill. The mill processes the wheat into flour, which is then used to make bread, which is then sold at the store. From seed to bread, at each step in the process, someone adds value through specialized knowledge and skills. One way to retain some of this added value is by processing the raw resources locally.

Unfortunately, the costs involved in establishing a full-scale processing facility can be substantial and out of reach for many communities. However, smaller-scale options exist, and through reinvestment into the business, gradual growth can occur. One of the first steps is to determine how existing resources in the community are typically transformed into processed goods. Another step is to determine the skills of available workers and how this knowledge can be exploited to take on some of the processing within the community. It is also necessary to determine outlets for distributing the processed product. Although national distribution through chain stores may be the ultimate goal, smaller specialty shops tend to be more receptive to carrying small quantities of products until the demand for the product and the supply capacity of the facility increases.

For example, perhaps the main crop in a community is corn destined for human consumption. A small portion could perhaps be diverted to a small operation making products such as corn relish. With the availability of label printers at the home office, professional packaging can be achieved at a fairly low cost. Distributing the product to retail outlets in the region may begin simply, with the rental of a small truck.

The same small-scale beginnings can hold for forestry products. Industrial saw mills have enormous capacity but also high startup costs. However, companies such as Norwood Industries provide a range of portable saws and planers starting from around $15,000.[12] Further, because of their portable nature, a group of community members may be able to pool their resources and share equipment. While the capacity of these saws is insufficient to supply major retail stores, it is possible to find niche uses for the semi-finished boards. This can include serving local furniture makers or homebuilders with quality products.

Both of these examples share a common thread: prior to setting up a processing facility, it needs to be determined what markets local products can serve. This may require finding other people or organizations with a specific need, and working together to figure out how to best serve both parties. Furthermore, it may be helpful to investigate current trends to determine how they might be exploited. For example, organic produce is typically sold at a higher price than non-organically raised products, and there is a growing demand for products made using sustainable methods.[13] The environmental movement (e.g., "Think Globally, Act Locally") encourages people to buy products that are manufactured close to their communities, for instance to reduce transportation emissions.[14] All of these ideas can not only help determine a target market, but can serve as a basis for promoting local goods.

While starting an operation to process locally available resources might sound promising, many communities face the problem of not having any single investor willing to commit the required resources. In order to share the risks involved and reduce the required investments, a group of interested individuals can consider the benefits provided by a co-operative. Similar to a public corporation, a co-operative (or co-op) is "an autonomous association of persons united voluntarily to meet their common economic, social, and cultural needs and aspirations through a jointly owned and democratically controlled enterprise."[15] Using this type of business model can reduce the risks involved in starting a new operation. First, the actual financial costs can be distributed widely. Second, this distributed ownership also means that the new venture can be *supplemental* to other sources of income. In other words, if a single individual tries to start a new processing operation, that individual risks everything and must devote all his or her time to maintaining the business. By using a co-op model, individual operators can maintain their primary sources of income and divide the time needed for the new venture to become operational. As an added bonus, co-ops can provide a social benefit to communities by drawing them together under a single goal.

These ideas are primarily focused on establishing local forms of production. Encouraging an external operation to set up a facility in the community may provide an alternative option. Toyota is known for its efficient production and is an innovation leader, within and outside the automobile manufacturing industry. One of their business practices involves the co-location of plants in close geographic proximity to their suppliers. This practice allows Toyota to hold very little inventory by instead receiving smaller and more frequent deliveries from suppliers. This business model may also serve to optimize transportation costs. Rather than transferring bulky unfinished goods to a plant and subsequently transporting the finished products to distributors, the costs associated with the first step are eliminated. Using these ideas, it may be worthwhile to have a community member look for and contact larger companies which process the region's resources to determine whether a processing plant can be developed in the local area.

SAME BUSINESS, DIFFERENT CUSTOMERS

As described earlier, when considering how to derive more value from local resources, one option is to think about how those resources are currently being used. Another option is to consider complementary or substitute resources. Familiarity and inertia often keep communities on a single path, doing things because "that is how we've always done them." For example, a farmer may have a certain rotation of crops for his or her fields, based on the soil and water conditions. That same farmer will likely have an existing outlet (or multiple customers) for each of the harvests. In such cases, it may be of some value to consider what *else* could be planted that may yield a higher return on the crop. Furthermore, are there other uses for the crop? Could these alternative uses may pay more for the harvest?

If a business is raising livestock, there may be other animals that can be raised instead of (or in addition to) those currently being raised. In both cases, it is important to look at trends in society and to anticipate how people's needs and preferences are changing. From an animal husbandry perspective, alpacas are a relatively new addition to Canadian farms (the first animals arrived in Canada in 1992) and their local presence has spawned a number of new outlets for their fibre.[16] Likewise, Stirling, Ontario farmers Martin Littkemann and Lori Smith found a niche market raising water buffalo to supply Canadian producers of buffalo mozzarella cheese.[17]

From a forestry perspective, the same ideas hold. While crops and animals reach maturity and harvesting much faster than trees, a forward-looking policy can still be beneficial. When replanting trees, it may be worth considering whether or not a different species may lead to increased future options for the harvested product. The difficulty is balancing short-term needs with long-term gains. For instance, some hardwoods, like oak, may take anywhere from 70–120 years to mature, while poplar can be harvested after forty years.[18]

Four key strategies can be considered:

- Identify the ways in which local, available natural resources *can* be processed.
- Take stock of local resources, including the skill sets of available employees, and determine what the community *could* produce.
- Find a match between local resources, available skills in the community, and where potential customers see value.
- When looking at commercial production, start small, and aim for growth.

Case Study – Ontario Water Buffalo Company

Company Overview and Background

In 2006, four years after switching from dairy to beef production, Martin Littkemann and Lori Smith were looking for a creative way to use their farm in Stirling, Ontario beyond cattle and cash crops. Following a friend's suggestion, they began researching the commercial potential of producing water buffalo milk, a product used around the world but virtually unheard of in North America. By 2008, they had purchased their first heifers, and today the Ontario Water Buffalo Company's production of water buffalo milk is thriving, supplying the fast-growing artisan cheese industry. Ontario Water Buffalo Company's success has stemmed from being at the forefront of a new Canadian market. Because bufala cheese is a high-end product in Canada, Martin and Lori did extensive front-end research to ensure their buffalo products would meet the most stringent standards. This began with fact-finding trips to learn production methods and purchase a top-quality breed. After purchasing an initial thirty-nine heifers and one bull, they are now developing their own custom breed.

As they built their herd, they concurrently networked with local cheese producers. They found greatest interest amongst Italian cheese producers in Toronto already producing cow-based mozzarella products. Ultimately, Ontario Water Buffalo Co. built a strong partnership with Quality Cheese in Vaughan, who were already importing buffalo mozzarella from Italy and had an established distribution network intact. With the support of University of Guelph researcher Art Hill, they settled on an artisanal recipe, as industrial techniques would not produce a high-quality cheese.

Two years later, Ontario Water Buffalo Company is one of two farms supplying Quality Cheese. Their milk is used to produce five different varieties of *bufala* cheese, including mozzarella, bocconcini, and ricotta.

Fast Facts

Ontario Water Buffalo Company
http://www.ontariowaterbuffalo.com

Location: Stirling, Hastings County, Ontario

Key Products: Water buffalo milk for cheese production

Success Factors:
- First mover advantage
- Untapped niche market
- Premium product
- Use of existing infrastructure
- Industry partnerships

Potential for Growth:
- Expansion into water buffalo meat market domestically and through exports

Their products are sold directly to restaurants, and to individual consumers through select grocers in Toronto and Quality's own factory store. Initially, transportation proved to be an issue; however, Quality invested in a refrigerated truck to transport the milk from Hastings to Toronto. Quality's willingness to develop the transportation infrastructure is a symbol of the long-term nature of the partnership between the two firms and the shared commitment to build this new local cheese market. Given that the less-fresh Italian product costs more than $20/kg for transportation alone, this local network has significant competitive advantages in both cost and quality.

Key Success Factors

Ontario Water Buffalo Co. offers several key lessons to other small rural businesses:

1 First Mover Advantage

In converting their farm from beef to water buffalo milk, Martin and Lori have been true pioneers in Ontario's agricultural landscape. Ontario Water Buffalo Co. has been able to develop a strong partnership with Quality Cheese, which has in turn led to the release of Ontario's first *bufala* cheese products. As others come to market, Quality's product will be the benchmark. Likewise, other cheese makers will likely look to Ontario Water Buffalo Co. as a first choice for their milk supply because of their established reputation. Because they have borne the risk of venturing into untested markets, they have a distinct advantage as the market grows.

2 Untapped Niche Market

Ontario Water Buffalo Co.'s move into the *bufala* cheese product market was a highly strategic one. Ontario's large Italian communities, combined with broader society's knowledge of and demand for quality Italian foods, meant there was already demand for buffalo mozzarella cheese. The local Italian cheese production and distribution network meant that it would be relatively simple to get the end product into the customer's hands. By building the right partnerships, Martin and Lori were able to produce a high-quality, domestic product that drastically undercut the price of existing imported products.

Their goal is for the business to move beyond the current niche so that their product can be adopted widely. While provincial policy does not yet regulate water buffalo milk according to the standards of cow and goat milk, Ontario Water Buffalo Co. already produces their products in compliance with stringent cow milk regulations. They are also engaged in lobbying the government to recognize their product under the Milk Act.

3 Premium Product

Critical to the success of their new venture has been the high quality of Martin and Lori's buffalo milk. Because the milk is used to create a high-end product it is critical to maintain stringent quality controls. Their business set-up was thus designed to maximize product quality. This involved attending global forums, integrating custom research from a leading agricultural university, learning from established international players, and working with supply chain partners to ensure quality throughout the process.

The product also offers unique health benefits compared to traditional cow's milk. This helps appeal to "foodies," a key target group composed of consumers interested in how their food is produced, "from field to fork." This group tends to value foods produced locally and, because they associate local food production with quality, is willing to pay more for such products.

4 Use of Existing Infrastructure

Martin and Lori overcame a significant barrier to entry by using their existing farm land and equipment to launch this new product. This significantly reduced the start-up costs. Further, their knowledge of farming and breeding has been an invaluable asset in launching this new venture.

Future Opportunities

While the water buffalo milk business has proved lucrative for Martin and Lori, buffalo must be bred regularly to continue milk production. Inevitably, Ontario Water Buffalo Co. ends up with male calves for which there is currently no market. This surplus does, however, offer an opportunity for additional growth.

Presently there are no suppliers of water buffalo meat in Canada and only a small number in the United States. Compared to beef, water buffalo meat has approximately 32% less cholesterol, 93% less saturated fat, 55% fewer calories, and 9% more protein. In addition to the nutritional benefits of water buffalo meat, many prefer the product for its mild flavour and soft texture.[A] Water buffalo production further requires minimal pesticide use, antibiotics, and growth hormones compared to beef production.[B] The market for buffalo meat has high growth potential as a result of the product's health benefits and superior production process in relation to beef. The physical composition of water buffalo meat is very similar to beef, so it provides similar cuts useful for steaks, roasts, burgers, and sausages.

Although there is currently no established water buffalo meat market in Canada, substantial markets do exist in Italy and Brazil. The American market is also in early stages of development. The benefits of the product, as well as Ontario Water Buffalo Co.'s production methods, make it a competitive product for key target markets.

Conclusions

In Ontario Water Buffalo Co., Martin and Lori have built an innovative rural farming enterprise. By developing a unique, high-quality product and working with an established business partner to take it to market, this new venture has experienced steady growth. To continue their growth, they can explore the market for water buffalo meat in Ontario. By utilizing their core strengths and effectively targeting influential market segments, Ontario Water Buffalo Company is likely to continue to be a key player in this emerging industry.

A "ME Water Buffalo Co." Accessed Nov. 28, 2009. *Local Harvest*, http://www.localharvest.org/farms/M32328.

B Antonio, Borghese, *Buffalo Production and Research* (Rome: Food and Agricultural Organization of the UN, 2007).

SUMMARY

An important approach for rural community revitalization involves capitalizing on the skilled trades sector. New technology advancements in traditional resource-based and manufacturing industries require a workforce that has a more highly developed skill base. Additionally, businesses seeking new site locations in rural communities often require a stable workforce that is skilled in trades. Working at the local or regional levels, CED practitioners should encourage municipalities to take stock of current and future employment needs – and to partner with educational institutions – to grow the awareness of the importance of the skilled trades sector in the new rural economy.

CED professionals can also use a variety of strategies to encourage current businesses to explore new value-added aspects. It is important to work with municipal leaders and staff to remove unnecessary barriers to new processes, thereby supporting and encouraging existing businesses to expand their size and scope.

8

Capitalizing on Tourism

As described in Chapter 7, agritourism is an increasingly successful form of value-added agriculture. As a whole, tourism is an important sector in Ontario's economy, contributing approximately $22 billion in revenue in 2007 alone. Composed primarily of small and medium-sized enterprises, the tourism industry is the largest employer of the province's youth. Investments in tourist attractions pay off not only in terms of direct employment and revenue, but also indirectly in terms of supporting the growth of associated industries, such as transportation, and the construction of vital infrastructure. In acknowledgment of the tourism industry's significance to the province, the Ontario government released a tourism competitiveness study in 2009, entitled: *Discovering Ontario: A Report on the Future of Tourism*. The Ontario government is implementing a number of the report's key recommendations, including:

1   *Creating Tourism Regions*: thirteen new tourism regions have been established across Ontario. Each Regional Tourism Organization (RTO) is independent, industry-led and not-for-profit. The RTOS are responsible for building and supporting competitive and sustainable tourism regions to attract more visitors, generate more economic activity, and create more jobs across the province. The intent behind this initiative is to enhance the coordination of tourism marketing and management. Each region works towards creating a unique brand and experience within a broader provincial brand, and there will be one destination marketing and management organization for each region, providing more voice and resources to local tourism initiatives.

Tourism Resources

Federal and provincial governments offer resources to assist in developing local and regional tourism programs and opportunities. Examples are provided below.

• **Ontario Culinary Tourism Alliance**

http://ontarioculinary.com

This alliance provides a number of resources related to the complete culinary tourism supply chain including research, best practice summaries, and case studies.

• **Ontario Ministry of Tourism Research**

www.mtc.gov.on.ca/en/publications/publications.shtml

The research section in the Ontario Ministry of Tourism's website contains reports and executive summaries profiling travel segments and tourist activities. It provides information about Canadian and US travelers to Ontario, as well as particular activities including agritourism, canoeing, and shopping.

• **Ontario Tourism Marketing Partnership Corp.**

http://www.tourismpartners.com

The Ontario Tourism Marketing Partnership Corporation (OTMPC) offers a wide range of programs to assist communities in developing tourist attractions. These programs include advertising, product development, consumer information services, as well as access to travel publications, and travel trade and media relations. Partnering with OTMPC may help a community reach markets that would otherwise be too difficult or expensive to target. The partnership goal is to "bring 'top-of-mind' awareness to your product or service while positioning Ontario as a premier four-season travel destination."

• **Ontario: Yours to Discover**

http://www.ontariotravel.net

This tourism website has sections on a number of regions in Ontario. Within the Eastern Ontario section, it hosts information on attractions along the St. Lawrence Seaway, as well as in the Quinte region and Prince Edward and Lennox-Addington counties. This section of the website also links to other sites, including www.realontario.ca, that profile additional regions and attractions within Eastern Ontario, as well as sites for the Prince Edward County and Quinte West Chambers of Commerce. While it is beneficial to promote tourist offerings

on as many relevant websites as possible, obtaining a posting
on an *aggregator* site (such as Ontario's official website), which
tourists are more likely to visit, should be a priority.
• **Rural Economic Development Programs, Tools and
Resources**
http://www.omafra.gov.on.ca/english/rural/edr/index.html
Provided by the Ontario Ministry of Rural Affairs, this website
assists with identifying local priorities and carrying out strategies to achieve a community's goals.

2 *Helping Operators Access Capital*: Ontario is helping to support
loans and/or loan guarantees to small and medium-sized tourism
operators working with existing lenders.

3 *Improving Way-Finding*: Ontario is installing better signage to
help make the province more welcoming, safe, and comfortable.

4 *Increasing E-Marketing and Online Booking*: Ontario is working
with industry to make it easier for travellers to book accommodations and visit attractions.[1]

This chapter highlights many initiatives that regions and local
communities can carry out to promote tourism. It includes information on how to identify tourism opportunities, particularly year-
round ones, as well as what tourists are looking for in a vacation.
It also explores how communities can effectively target key tourist
markets.

TOURISM OPPORTUNITIES IN LOCAL RESOURCES

While some regions are fortunate enough to possess natural wonders
and fascinating historical sites, others are not so privileged. Regardless of which category a region may fall into, a key aspect of tourism
is making the most of local resources and presenting them to potential tourists in a compelling, differentiated way.

Regional Resources

An important first step in identifying tourism opportunities in a
region is performing a resource inventory. This entails account-

ing for natural (lakes, trails, etc.), physical (lodging, restaurants, historical sites, etc.), human (artists, guides, etc.), relational (community linkages, business associations, etc.), and other potentially relevant resources that may play a role in the delivery of a tourist experience. As a part of this process, the community needs to define who and what constitutes its region. Is this a tourism initiative for a town, a county, or a more broadly defined area? Who can contribute resources, and who hopes to benefit?

As the community inventories local resources and answers these questions, the non-exhaustive set of potential tourist activities identified below can encourage creative thinking.

Culture and Entertainment
Historical Sites, Museums,
    and Art Galleries
Shopping and Dining
Aboriginal Cultural
    Experiences
Fairs and Festivals
Science and Technology
    Exhibits
Theme Parks and Exhibits
High Art Performances
Pro, Semi-Pro, International
    Sporting Events
Live Theatre
Literary or Film Festivals
Tastings
Spas
Casinos
Participatory Historical
    Activities
Equestrian and Western
    Events
Agritourism
Garden Theme Attractions
Comedy Festivals and Clubs

Outdoor and Activities
Golfing
Hunting
Fishing
Wildlife Viewing
Hiking, Climbing, and
    Paddling
Boating, Swimming, and Other
    Beach Activities
Sailing and Surfing
Exercising and Jogging
Cycling
Motorcycling
Horseback Riding
Snowmobiling and ATVing
Skiing, Snowboarding, and
    Snowshoeing
Wilderness Activities
Skating
Team Sports
Sports and Games, Amateur
    Tournaments
Musical Concerts, Festivals,
    and Attractions

In considering a region's resources, a community can ask which of these activities can be offered; are there other offerings it can deliver;

and, is there anything it can offer uniquely, compared to other communities. This may require research to identify the tourist attractions available elsewhere in the region or province. If there is one activity, or grouping of similar activities, which a region can uniquely offer to tourists, it may serve to become an important part of the branding strategy. For example, the town of Almonte promotes itself as Canada's Festival Capital, while Lennox and Addington County touts itself as having some of Eastern Ontario's most spectacular views. While the two communities surely have other tourist attractions, these specific features are made salient in their branding efforts because they present a relatively differentiated image.

Off-season Opportunities

An important factor to consider when performing a tourism resource inventory is seasonality. Are the local resources accessible year-round, or only in the summer or winter? Attracting tourists throughout off-peak and shoulder seasons may be a challenge, but the creative leveraging of resources and the intentional construction of off-peak attractions, even if they are only one-off events, may help. If a region is home to a lake, can it serve as a site for a golden years pond hockey tournament, outdoor curling bonspiel, or a polar bear club swim? Members of the community often provide a wealth of ideas. Events that the community is interested in supporting, such as an amateur animal tracking competition or a weekly improvisational show, will have greater potential to blossom into off-season tourist attractions for the region.

As idea starters, some examples of all-season or off-season tourist attractions include:

- Niagara's Ice Wine Festival (January)
- Friends of Frontenac Provincial Park Winter Camping and Wilderness Skills Program (January/February)
- Belleville Kids' Ice Fishing Day (February)
- Ontario Science Centre's Family Day Sleepover (February)
- Bronte Creek Provincial Park's Maple Syrup Festival (March)
- Cross Quetico Lakes Skiing, Mushing, Skijoring Tour (March)
- Welland's Little NHL Hockey Tournament (March)
- Swiss Hill Inn's Gem and Hard Rock Tour (Year-Round)
- Ste. Anne's Spa Girlfriends Getaway (Year-Round)

More creative idea starters for year-round tourism can be found at http://www.ontariotravel.net.

TOURISM OPPORTUNITIES IN CUSTOMER DESIRES

In addition to thinking about what the region can offer, the needs and wants of your target market should also be considered. Unfortunately, the expression "if you build it, they will come," does not always reflect reality. Individuals have a variety of reasons for visiting particular tourist sites or regions that depend on their life stage, ambitions, hobbies, peer groups, etc. A recent government-sponsored study identified tourists' general motivations for taking a vacation.[2] These motivations are listed in order from most to least frequently cited:

- Get a break from the day-to-day environment
- Relax and relieve stress
- Enrich relationship with spouse/children
- Create lasting memories
- Keep family ties alive
- Have a life with no fixed schedule
- See or do something different
- Enrich one's perspective on life
- Gain knowledge
- Renew connections with people
- Stimulate the mind
- Be physically challenged
- Have stories to share back home
- Be pampered
- Seek solitude and isolation

These motivations show what tourists hope to derive from their experience. For example, they go to museums to gain knowledge and spas to be pampered. As such, it is important to keep the target audience's desires in mind when planning, promoting, and executing a tourist experience. However, the same experience (e.g., a winter wilderness skills course) may provide different benefits to different target groups. For example, a single, middle-aged man may enroll in a winter wilderness skills course to take a break, gain knowledge, and be physically challenged, while a family may enroll in a similar course to enrich intra-family relationships, create memories, and obtain stories to share back home. One risk in branding is that in trying to be all things to all people a brand might end up appealing to no one. Recognizing this, it is important to have a clear idea of who you are targeting with your tourist initiative and what their motivations are likely to be for coming to your region.

DESTINATION CHARACTERISTICS

Destination characteristics also play a role in tourists' decisions about where to vacation. As such, it is relevant to understand what is most important to a potential target group, and enhance alignment between visitor desires and the community's offerings. Some destination characteristics include:

- Feeling safe
- No health concerns
- Convenient access by car, train, bus, etc.
- Lots for adults to see and do
- Lots for children to see and do
- Information about the destination online
- Low-cost package deals
- Familiarity with the culture and language
- Great shopping opportunities
- Having friends or relatives there
- Catering to disabled persons
- Very different culture

While some of these characteristics may fall outside the community's realm of influence (e.g., being culturally different), others may be addressable, potentially making local initiatives more appealing to tourists. Can perceptions of safety with riskier activities be increased (e.g., in whitewater rafting)? Can access be improved by offering shuttle buses for a winter festival? Can pre-arranged value packages be offered, such as horseback riding, dinner at a farm, and lodging at a bed-and-breakfast? Can online reservations be accepted? Taking care of such details will not only enhance the attractiveness of a destination, but also increase the likelihood that tourists will experience their desired vacation benefits.

Successful tourism initiatives effectively leverage local resources to meet visitors' needs. As many vacationers' destination options are boundless, it is important to think about what makes an offering different and to whom this point of difference might be compelling. As such, this process involves not only reflecting on local assets, but also on other destinations' offerings, as well as consumers' desires.

TARGETING TOURISM INITIATIVES

At some point after cataloguing the region's resources and considering potential tourist offerings, it is important to consider whom the community wants to target. The objective is to identify types of people who are most likely to come to the region based on local tourist offerings, although, in an iterative process, the local offerings may evolve once a target market has been selected. Who might local offerings appeal to most? A recent Environics study, *Ontario Tourism Marketing Partnership Segmentation*,[3] which profiles different segments of people who vacation in Ontario, notes that almost 60 per cent of Ontarians travel within the province for pleasure, and that about 10 per cent of Americans within close proximity of the border also vacation in Ontario (unfortunately, no data regarding other Canadians are included in the report).

The study, which can be consulted for greater detail, provides segment information on both Ontarians and Americans who vacation in the province. These types of people could be included in a community program's target market analysis. The study identifies several key market segments:[4]

- *Upscale Adventurers*: Financially secure older middle-aged married couples with adult-age children (some are empty nesters)
- *Provincial Families*: Financially secure younger and middle-aged suburban and ex-urban families with lots of children
- *Young Go-Goes*: Young, successful, well-off, multi-ethnic, urban trendsetters
- *Retired Roamers*: Midscale mature and older retirees and seniors living in suburbia and towns
- *High Flyers*: Mix of wealthy older families and married couples without children at home
- *Footloose Families*: Middle-class households with large, younger families, working hard to live the "American Dream"

- *Silver Streaks*: Mature, middle-class, married couples who have already raised their families (some widows and widowers)
- *Young and Restless*: Well-educated younger singles in smaller childless households.

After studying these segment profiles, described in greater detail in Appendix F, it may be clear that some categories better align with local resources and potential tourist offerings than others. As a result, promotions can strategically target one or more of these groups. The target markets should be kept in mind when developing the tourist offering, branding it, and deciding how to position it in promotions. It is important to consider individuals' motivations for travelling and how the community can fulfill their needs and wants.

One caveat with regards to these segment profiles is that they are broad composites, created to help make sense of the different types of people who travel in Ontario for leisure. There are sub-groups within these constructed groupings, which may have more specific defining characteristics. Additionally, at the individual level, each person's needs and wants will vary somewhat from the overriding segment description, and may evolve over time depending on changes in their life contexts. Consequently, simply because an offering is not a *key leisure activity* for a segment group as a whole at the present time, does not mean it will fail to find interest from some people within that segment, or even those not in any of the segments described above.

These segments comprise a large number of people, and if the objective is to attract a few thousand additional visitors per year, appealing to a subset of a segment may still help a community meet its goals. For more information on leisure travelers in Ontario, the full version of the Environics report *Ontario Tourism Marketing Partnership Segmentation Summary*, is available on the Ontario Ministry of Tourism Research website, or through the Ontario Tourism Marketing Partnership Corporation.

REACHING A TARGET MARKET

Once a tourism target market has been selected, the community's uniquely positioned offering must be communicated. Different segments may be more or less receptive to certain approaches (e.g., a rational information-based approach vs. an emotional imagery-based approach) and certain channels (e.g., advertising via the Internet vs. visitor centre brochures).

It is important to consistently reach a target market with a unique and personally appealing message because approximately half (49 per cent) of Canadian tourists to Ontario already have a destination in mind when they start to plan their vacation.[5] Thus, brand awareness is integral to attracting tourists to a community. Some other ways tourists select their destinations involve starting with a certain type of vacation experience in mind and doing research (23 per cent), or starting with specific activities in mind and doing research (14 per cent). This suggests that it is also imperative to have a presence in those places where your target market obtains vacation planning information.

Generally, these are the sources that people consult when planning a trip (listed from more to less frequently consulted):[5]

- An Internet website
  - Website of a hotel or resort
  - A tourism website of a country, region, or city
  - A travel planning/booking website
  - A website of an attraction
  - Other related websites
- Advice of others/word of mouth
- Past experience/been there before
- A travel agent
- Maps
- Official travel guides or brochures from province
- Visitor information centres
- Articles in newspapers or magazines
- An auto club such as CAA
- Advertisements in newspapers or magazines
- Travel guide books, such as Fodor's
- Travel information received in the mail
- Programs on television
- An electronic newsletter or magazine received by email
- Advertisements on television
- Visits to trade, travel, or sports shows

Given the Internet's place at the top of the list, constructing a website and associating it with the provincial tourism website, and any regional tourism websites should be a fundamental component of a promotional plan. Appealing to peoples' desires to travel, and ensuring a good fit between the promotion and execution of the tourist offering, should contribute positively to the next two items: word of mouth and past experience. This should lead to return travel. Developing other less critical sources of information can be explored to help further a community's potential to reach its target market(s).

Ultimately, the process of reaching out to a target market occurs much later in the process after the tourism offering (or product) has been conceptualized and developed, and a strategy, in terms of segmenting, targeting, positioning, and branding, has been defined.

Targeting is powerful because it has the potential to provide mutual benefits; it promotes the efficient use of resources and promises to better meet the needs of consumers. For example, in Eastern Ontario, there are a number of segments, comprising people from Ontario and beyond, which could be targeted for a tourism program. Notably, people in some of these segments appear more likely than people in others to enjoy the available tourist offerings. Investigating these segments further would likely provide an even better sense of their travel motivations, preferences, and sources of vacation information.

SUMMARY

Rural communities are rich in cultural, heritage, and natural assets providing key ingredients for tourism attraction. Completing the asset inventory described in Part 1 provides a key base of knowledge for the development of a tourism strategy. Local municipal and business leaders may require support to analyze potential tourism options and markets prior to embarking on an advertising campaign. As many tourism operators are small business owners, they may also benefit from opportunities to learn about social media marketing techniques. CED practitioners should promote networking and collaborative efforts among local and regional businesses to increase the potential for tourism to revitalize rural economies.

PART FOUR

Supporting and Sustaining the New Rural Economy

Across rural Canada, economic, cultural, institutional, and demographic changes challenge community leaders. Individual communities and regions struggle to create a sustainable future. In some areas, investments in infrastructure do not appear adequate to support the new rural economy.

Infrastructure is most often defined as visible community assets: the transportation systems that move people, goods, and services, the bricks and mortar educational and health institutions that bring value to the community, and the emerging infrastructure of information and communications technology. Technological and societal advances have refined our thinking about infrastructure requirements and investments. The definition of "community infrastructure" has evolved to include the social infrastructure that supports local economies. Medical and health services, recreational assets – both built and natural – and cultural infrastructure, such as faith-based institutions and arts amenities, increasingly factor into the decisions about relocating a business or a family. A broad range of amenity assets can be significant whether one is a young professional, has a family, is looking for a retirement location, or is interested in visiting as a tourist.

Infrastructure investments are a key component of economic development. As discussed in Chapter 6, either on their own or as part of a regional effort, rural community leaders are considering new ways to support the development of creative economies. Financial constraints need to be addressed; CED professionals often work to provide greater access to capital funds to better support the businesses and entrepreneurs that make up the creative class. Today, most municipalities also face the need for significant reinvestment into their existing infrastructures of transportation and water treatment systems. Rural municipalities located near urban centres experience significant development and new settlement pressures. While this population increase expands the municipal tax base, it often adds fiscal pressures because of the need to provide new services, such as libraries and recreation facilities. Conversely, other rural municipalities facing population decline struggle to maintain their existing services and heritage elements.

Part 4 explores the components of community infrastructure in the context of economic development, and especially in light of new rural economy options. Questions and key issues raised by community leaders across Eastern and Southwestern Ontario set the context. Among the questions addressed are: "what community attributes attract businesses?", "what rural business financing models exist?", and "how can rural communities support the emerging creative economy?"

Recognizing that technology plays a key role, Chapter 9, Technology as the Foundation, documents the importance of a high-speed communications infrastructure for growing and sustaining rural economies. Expanding from the traditional notion of infrastructure, Chapter 10 considers a broader definition of healthcare that is emerging, as well as focuses on strategies for community use in attracting physicians to rural practices. New and innovative approaches for investment attraction are outlined in Chapter 11. This chapter references a number of infrastructure studies documenting growing investment gaps and challenges in rural municipalities. The new rural economy challenges entrepreneurs, community leaders, and policy makers to explore a wider range of options for financing creative industries and professions. New investment approaches, as well as shifts in policy at all government levels, are required to fully realize the potential of this new economic paradigm. Finally, Chapter 12, Goods, Services, and People Movement, explores the importance and impact of transportation systems on the new rural economy and outlines challenges that municipalities face in allocating scarce resources to this important aspect of economic development.

9

Technology as the Foundation

Economic vitality in rural areas demands high-speed broadband Internet access, particularly in developing high-value sectors like the creative economy. In seeking to overcome economic downturns, governments around the world have made providing broadband access a priority, in some instances recognizing it as a basic human right.[1] Various government economic stimulus packages have invested in creating far-reaching networks to satisfy this objective.

THE NEED FOR BROADBAND INTERNET ACCESS

The Internet has become a primary means for personal and business communication, information exchange, and learning. However, rural communities can lack reliable Internet access. This poses a serious, detrimental hindrance to their sustainability and growth.

Statistics Canada defines "rural and small town" as those regions outside the commuting zones of centres with populations of 10,000 or more. The May 10, 2010 Statistics Canada Daily noted a persistent digital divide between rural and urban communities. Between 2007 and 2009, Internet usage was at least ten percentage points lower in rural communities than in urban areas.[2] Industry Canada's National Broadband Maps provide a more detailed understanding.[3] The maps show the number of either un-served or under-served households per 25 km², represented as hexagonal areas. Examining the maps indicates that, in Canada in 2009, there were still areas of over 800 households without broadband access.

To address this issue, in 2009, the Canadian Government made connecting rural Canadians part of its Economic Action Plan stimulus initiative, allocating $225 million over three years. Since then, several key projects have taken off through the *Broadband Canada* program, with one recent round of projects promising connectivity to a further 30,000 households nationwide.[4] Other government initiatives, including the *Rural Connections Broadband Program* from the Ontario Ministry of Rural Affairs (OMRA) have also contributed to extending broadband coverage to rural communities. *Rural Connections* alone has contributed over $10.6 million in eastern Ontario since its inception in 2007. The Eastern Ontario Regional Network (EORN) was launched by the Eastern Ontario Wardens Caucus (EOWC) to extend broadband to 95 per cent of rural Eastern Ontario. EORN has now accessed *Broadband Canada* funding, as well as matching support from OMRA and local municipalities, for a large-scale, regional project to extend broadband availability throughout eastern Ontario.

TECHNOLOGIES FOR AFFORDABLE BROADBAND INTERNET

A broadband network usually involves two parts: a backhaul and an access network. The backhaul is the main network, akin to large highways. The access network connects individual homes or small communities to the larger backhaul, much like local streets connect to larger highways. Fibre is usually utilized in the backhaul as it provides the greatest bandwidth and highest reliability. It relies on pulsated lasers to relay data for very long distances through very thin strands of high-quality glass. These advantages, however, come at the high costs of extending the fibers through varying terrain. The backhaul includes many points of presence (PoP), which are access points to which a household can be directly attached.

There are several traditional technologies that can be utilized in creating a broadband access network:

- Wired technologies tend to be reliable, but are costly to install in areas with low population density:
  - Fibre optic cable is highly reliable and has the greatest capacity for transferring data.

- ◦ Coaxial broadband utilizes the same infrastructure used by cable TV, a technology not generally available in rural communities.
- ◦ DSL (Digital Subscriber Line) communicates over regular phone lines but uses dedicated modems. DSL differs from dial-up Internet access in that it utilizes non-audible frequencies, so as not to interfere with regular phone operation.
- Wireless technologies have been easier to install in rural communities because they require a smaller infrastructure investment:
  - ◦ In recent years, 3G cellular has become widely used, allowing transmission of large multimedia files; however, there are significant coverage gaps in rural Canada. Adoption of 3G cellular in rural areas is restricted by the technology's limited capability in providing true broadband, in addition to relatively high subscription costs.
  - ◦ Fixed wireless is another alternative that relies on what is called line of sight (LoS) communication. This option offers a substantial capacity advantage over 3G cellular and at a more affordable cost. The LoS nature of deployment, however, limits the applicability of fixed wireless technology to flat terrains with minimal physical obstruction. Certain weather conditions may also interfere with the operation of fixed wireless networks.
  - ◦ Wi-Fi is a popular technology that transfers data wirelessly from specially-installed transmission towers. A limitation, however, is that each tower has to be within the radio communication range of the next tower.
  - ◦ Satellite broadband is usually reserved for areas where using other technologies is prohibitively costly or physically unviable.

The EORN initiative in rural Eastern Ontario is technology neutral, and is guided by the performance of proposed technologies. This approach permits EORN to utilize several technologies including fibre, terrestrial wireless (Wi-Fi), and satellite, to maximize the reach of broadband throughout the diverse geographies of the region, and allow for increased competition and improved end-user service. Depending on the applicability of each technology to the area of deployment, EORN accommodates any alternative for rural broadband that satisfies the project requirements.

NON-TRADITIONAL ALTERNATIVES FOR ACCESSIBLE
NETWORKS

The recent surge of interest in providing rural broadband has brought to light other, non-traditional alternatives for creating access networks that are affordable to both install and operate. These technologies are briefly discussed below. It should be noted, however, that these technologies are not applicable in all contexts. For example, the broadband over power lines option discussed below is not an applicable option for the Eastern Ontario region.

Broadband over Power Lines (BPL)

In December 2010, the Institute for Electrical and Electronics Engineers (IEEE) released standards for providing broadband Internet over power lines.[5] This has accelerated the testing and commercialization of Power Line Communications (PLC) that facilitate both creating power grids and broadband Internet access. Since BPL relies on an already existing infrastructure, deployment costs are substantially reduced; the power grid's minimal downtimes also produce a highly reliable network.

Wireless Mesh Networks (WMNs)

A network is often described as a mesh of nodes, or intersections, usually connected by wires. Over the past decade, several networking and communication advances have made wirelessly meshing network nodes possible. The resulting WMNs have shown great promise as a networking strategy that is easy to deploy and manage, with a high resilience to failures. With careful design, WMNs can cover very large geographical areas.

Typically, a home connects to the Internet either directly through a PoP by installing fibre optic cable directly to the house, or indirectly through DSL, BPL, or a similar service. Wi-Fi has emerged as a popular application of WMNs, providing broadband access without an investment in wired infrastructure to the home. Wi-Fi technology has also been widely standardized by the IEEE, providing Internet Service Providers (ISPs) with clear network traffic guidelines.[6] This provides end users with reliable, predictable service. While Wi-Fi is often associated with short-range coverage (ten metres or less), it can

---

Larissa, Greece – BPL in Action
Broadband over Power Lines (BPL) has had several successful trials. One early hybrid solution employing both wireless and BPL technologies (W/BPL) was successfully installed in Larissa, Greece.* Initially, the network was designed for more intelligent power regulation to handle outages in the summer due to the extensive use of irrigation pumps. This project required establishing robust communication over the power lines. Because this communication requirement only used 10 per cent of the network's capacity, it was decided to explore the possibility of providing broadband access through the power grid as well. The network provided broadband to over 600 inhabitants using BPL to connect to a PoP on the existing, traditional backhaul. "Last-mile" access to those still unreached by BPL was then facilitated through Wi-Fi.

* Sarafi, Tsiropoulos and Cottis, "Hybrid Wireless-Broadband over Power Lines: A Promising Broadband Solution in Rural Areas," IEEE *Communications Magazine*, November 2009.

---

also be applied to cover a large geographic area, thus becoming part of a backhaul network.

Cellular Broadband

Despite relatively high costs, cellular phones have enjoyed exponential growth in Canada over the past decade.[7] The introduction of smart phones, which allow cell phones to access multimedia over the Internet, has made broadband over cellular networks a trend that is expected to continue.[8] However, current cellular technologies, often referred to as 3G, are limited by high deployment costs for enhancing capacity or extending coverage. These costs have been an inhibiting factor in extending broadband cellular coverage to rural areas.

Several emerging networking technologies offer further options for expanding cellular network infrastructure:

- *Relay Stations* (RS), crudely speaking, are towers that connect wirelessly to cellular networks.[9] Cell phones can maintain service to a cellular network through up to two intermediary RSs. The cost of an RS is expected to be an order of magnitude less than that of a traditional wired cellular tower and RSs are expected to be easily, and cheaply, installed.
- *Femtocells* are similar to Wi-Fi access points except, instead of connecting to broadband backhaul, they connect to a cellular network. Thus, homeowners can plug femtocells to their home broadband connections and receive high-quality cellular service indoors.[10]

Indeed, many communication and networking technologies – both available and emerging – play a significant role in wireless broadband.[11] Many of these technologies are aimed directly at increasing broadband penetration at reduced costs for both the user and the provider.

REALIZING AND MAINTAINING BROADBAND AFFORDABILITY

In addition to installation and operating costs, several other cost factors need to be considered:

- Network planning considers factors such as the nature of the terrain where the access network is installed and the expected magnitude and nature of the network's traffic. A well-planned network is less prone to failures and requires minimal intervention.
- A growing best practice in network administration is that of installing a *self-healing* structure. Networks can be designed to recognize specific failure types and be able to prevent, correct, and/or adapt to the failure with minimal or no human intervention.
- As information and communication technologies (ICT) can create substantial energy losses, use of renewable energy sources can further minimize costs.[12] Energy sources such as solar panels and wind turbines can greatly reduce operational costs at both the backhaul and network access levels; WMNs, in particular, can be grid-independent for very long time periods.
- Beyond network and power considerations, once a network is installed, end-user affordability will be determined by ISP pricing.

In addition to supporting projects like EORN and SuperNET, governments must encourage and support ISP competition.

LEVERAGING RURAL BROADBAND

Rural areas offer a range of unique lifestyle options that are increasingly attractive to traditionally urban-based professionals. In attracting business development, as well as providing social services, the Internet is now a necessity rather than a luxury. Dependence on multimedia communications, especially applications like real-time video communication, is increasing. Access to broadband not only allows rural communities to acquire knowledge from around the world, but also to share their experiences, both personal and professional, with a wide audience.

Access to high-speed broadband Internet plays an important role in attracting and retaining rural youth. Reliable connectivity enables young people to readily obtain information, certification and knowledge, and maintain communication with their peers.

Provision of government services via the Internet can further require broadband usage. "E-government" services allow businesses and individuals to access government resources without having to travel long distances to central offices. Government use of online financial transactions provides an example to local businesses as to how they can use similar technologies securely and safely to expand their customer base. Broadband access can impact community health as well by providing easy access to health information, guiding patients to local clinics and hospitals, and allowing healthcare professionals to electronically transfer multimedia patient files and reports.

SUMMARY

Networks for delivering broadband Internet have a positive economic impact on rural areas.[13] They are the means, and not the end, to building stronger rural economies.[14] While governments should support building network infrastructure, it is important to ensure that market dynamics encourage Internet Service Providers to provide services at competitive rates.[15] Broadband penetration in rural areas further depends on recognizing how broadband connectivity can benefit the rural community, at personal, business, and collective levels.[16] CED professionals can help municipalities understand the language, opportunities, and challenges associated with information and communications technologies. They can also work with local institutions to ensure that ICT educational and training opportunities are made available to local businesses and the community at large so that the technology potential is understood and fully utilized.

10

The Economic Role of Healthcare

Economic development (CED) professionals understand the importance of healthcare systems and services to potential new residents
and businesses. "Is there a hospital?" "Can my family get a doctor?" "How far will I need to travel for specialist services?" These
are routine questions asked by people who are considering relocating. Rural communities in Canada face a shortage of physicians. A
recent study indicated that while 21 per cent of Canadians live in
rural areas, only 10 per cent of physicians practice in these areas.[1]
This shortage threatens not only the health and well-being of rural
residents, but also the communities' potential for economic growth.
Having an insufficient number of doctors makes it less attractive
for new residents to move to an area and for businesses to operate.
Conversely, having high-quality healthcare promotes a rural community's survival.

Increasingly, approaches to health and healthcare services are
evolving to include a broader range of models and professions
including Family Health Teams and Community Health Centres.
There is also a growing awareness of the important role of illness
and disease prevention through healthy lifestyle choices. Communities working to attract new employers and new resident populations
need to offer access to a comprehensive health system that includes
both infrastructure and professionals and a broad focus from wellness maintenance to illness treatment.

For many communities a basic step in growing this infrastructure is the recruitment of rural physicians. Below, we outline a range
of recruitment approaches. These can be tailored to attract other
healthcare professionals.

Rural Health and Economic Development
"Health is an extremely important issue for all Canadians. In rural and northern areas it is critically important from two perspectives – personal health and wellness, and the impacts that the presence or lack of healthcare has on regional economic development. Healthcare is one of the 'building blocks' for further economic development. Understanding the linkage between health provision and economic development is crucial to building vibrant, sustainable, and resilient communities."

Transforming Northern Health – Innovations Making a Difference – Rural Ontario Institute
April 2010, http://ruralontarioinstitute.ca

STRATEGIES TO GROW THE NUMBER OF RURAL PHYSICIANS

To effectively grow the number of rural physicians, a multi-pronged approach that considers both short-term and long-term strategies should be taken. In addition, strategies to increase the number of rural physicians can be targeted at practising physicians from outside the rural community, spouses and families of these physicians, medical students, and youth from rural areas. These strategies are outlined below.

Engage in Recruitment Initiatives

Community leaders can actively engage in initiatives to recruit physicians. Some communities have local recruitment committees and programs in place whereas others have human resource departments that are charged with this responsibility. In addition, a growing trend in Canada is for communities to hire a *community recruiter* whose job it is to recruit physicians on a part- or full-time basis.[2] Community recruiters are creative in the methods they use. These methods can also be used by communities that do not have the financial resources to hire recruiters. The following are activities and practices to consider:

- Use job fairs and workshops: Potential recruits can be found at job fairs and professional events. Participating in these events allows a CED practitioner to look for and establish relationships with these recruits (e.g., physicians and medical students).
- Introduce recruits to the community: Potential recruits often need an advance introduction to a rural area before they will consider practising there. Tours and recruitment events are effective ways of "selling" a community. Consider the following:
  - Events can highlight the attractions of the area and general benefits of living there such as a sense of warmth and community, a lack of traffic, and healthy outdoor activities.
  - Questions that concern the personal needs of potential recruits and their families should be addressed (e.g., employment needs of the spouse, educational needs of the children, and available housing).
  - Recruits want to know about their potential colleagues. One way of doing this is for practising physicians in the rural area to be invited. Physicians are more likely to move to a rural area if they know and get along with other clinicians in the community.
  - Potential recruits may be impressed if recruiters know a lot about them and their needs before a tour or visit. Recruiters can do this by communicating with recruits electronically and on the phone to get to know them and their family. In this way, recruiters can anticipate questions that recruits may have during a visit.
- Develop professional promotional materials: Potential recruits may learn about a rural community by reading promotional materials. It is important for these materials (e.g., brochures and websites) to be up-to-date and professionally designed.
- Foster word-of-mouth promotions by existing physicians: A potential recruit may become interested in a career in a rural area by interacting with physicians working in the area.[3] As much as possible, recruiters and community leaders should forge relationships with physicians currently practising locally. Rural physicians are community ambassadors who can convincingly highlight the benefits of working in a rural area.
- Pursue local talent: Medical students who are born and raised in rural communities are more likely to return to practise in a rural area. Recruiters should therefore try to maintain relationships with

these students when they are away from their home communities during their medical training. By keeping in touch, recruiters have increased opportunities to persuade these students to return to their home communities.

Create Financial Incentives

In the short term, financial incentives can help to attract physicians to rural areas. It is worthwhile to note, however, that the long-term efficacy of financial incentives has been found to be quite limited.[4] Nevertheless, financial incentives are typically an important component of physician recruitment programs. Such incentives include guaranteed minimum income contracts, isolation allowances, loan forgiveness, assistance with medical practice expenses, scholarships and bursaries for medical students, and signing bonuses.[5]

Recent examples of financial incentive programs include a program in British Columbia in which physicians were offered a $10,000 signing bonus to practise in underserviced areas. In addition, Ontario's Free Tuition Program has provided up to $40,000 to final-year medical students, residents, and recently graduated physicians in exchange for a return-of-service commitment. Also, in Eastern Ontario, the City of Quinte West's physician recruitment program offered $100,000 over five years to doctors who set up their practice in the Quinte West Medical Centre.[6]

When developing a funding model for physicians, several things should be taken into consideration:

- Financial incentives should provide security and flexibility (i.e., options) for the physician.
- Offering greater financial incentives may be appropriate if a physician is required to take on a higher level of clinical responsibility. This is often the case for rural physicians as they are frequently required to perform a greater number of procedures than their urban counterparts.
- Funding may be allocated for continuing medical education, such as attending conferences or taking courses. For example, part of Alberta's successful Rural Physician Action Plan (http://www. rpap.ab.ca/about/home.html) consisted of an Enrichment Program that allocated funds for physicians to upgrade existing skills to meet the needs of rural communities.[7]

- Last, as outlined above, a funding model should consider a physician's personal needs such as support for the physician's spouse and family.[8]

Engage in Community Development

A longer-term strategy that can be used to grow the number of physicians in a rural community is for leaders to engage in activities that make the community more attractive. CED practitioners can work in partnership with other community stakeholders (e.g., local residents, various organizations, physicians, and administrators of healthcare facilities) to design and implement community improvements that may help to meet a potential physician's professional and personal needs. Several questions to consider include:

- What is the state of the healthcare facilities in the area?
- Is there an opportunity for group practice in the community?
- Are there adequate recreation options?
- What initiatives are in place to help integrate physicians and their families into the community?
- How supportive is the community of spouses and children?
- What kinds of efforts are being made to develop healthcare grant proposals to bring additional resources to the community?

Expose Medical Students to Rural Practice

Exposure allows medical students to gain an appreciation for the attractions of a rural community and better understand what rural practice might be like. Accordingly, community leaders would benefit from establishing connections with medical school administrators to encourage an increase in the number of rural rotations that are offered to medical students. Community leaders can also encourage existing rural physicians to be educators in medical programs. As teachers, these rural physicians are role models who can positively influence students' attitudes towards rural practice.[9]

Get Rural Youth Interested in Medicine

A long-term strategy a community can use to grow their number of physicians is to encourage rural youth to become interested in

Online Resources for Healthcare Strategies
HealthKick Huron
http://www.healthkickhuron.ca
HealthKick Huron is an initiative that takes a multi-pronged approach to address the shortage of healthcare human resources. The project is based in Seaforth, Huron County, and co-located with the Huron Community Health Team and the Gateway Rural Research Institute. HealthKick Huron has won numerous awards for its innovation in health human resources.
Recruitment and Retention of Medical Doctors – Research Report
http://economicrevitalization.ca http://business.queensu.ca/centres/monieson/docs/client_research_reports/ Recruitment _ and_Retention_report.pdf
This research report addresses the recruitment and retention of physicians in Canada. The report was prepared for The Monieson Centre at Queen's School of Business by Dr. Gordon Hunter. In particular, the report focuses on identifying what motivates medical practitioners, and what may attract them to a rural area.
Rural Canada: Access to Healthcare – Research Report
http://publications.gc.ca/collections/Collection-R/LoPBdP/BP/prb0245-e.htm
This research report presents the issues and challenges of healthcare in rural Canada and examines the roles, both existing and potential, of the federal government. This research report was prepared by Stephen Hunter in the Economics Division of the Federal Government. It outlines strategies for the recruitment and retention of physicians in rural areas.
MedQUEST
Memorial University http://www.med.mun.ca/StudentAffairs/Med-Quest.aspx and
Schulich School of Medicine & Dentistry http://www.schulich.uwo.ca/swomen/medquest/
MedQUEST is a summer program for students in grades 10–12. It is a career-oriented program, specially designed for students in rural areas. During each MedQUEST session, students are introduced to a variety of health professions such as medicine,

nursing, pharmacy, occupational therapy, and physiotherapy. These health careers and special topics are presented through lectures, demonstrations, experiments, guest speakers, research projects, job shadowing, role playing, small group sessions, and tours of healthcare facilities.

Information on Physician Recruitment/Retention programs in eastern Ontario

County of Hastings Family Physician Recruitment Program
http://www.hastingscounty.com/index.php?option=com_docman&task=doc

City of Peterborough – Physician Recruitment
http://www.docfinder.ca

City of Quinte West Doctor Recruitment Program
http://www.city.quintewest.on.ca/en/business/Physician-Recruitment.asp

Renfrew County Physician Recruitment
http://www.renfrewareahealthvillage.ca/need_a_doctor.php

medicine. One innovative initiative that has done this is MedQUEST, a week-long summer camp that gives high school students from rural areas a taste of a healthcare career. Over the course of the week, students learn to deliver robotic babies, read x-rays, splint and cast fractures, perform simple sutures, give injections, and learn what it takes to become a physician.[10] Early exposure to the practice of medicine can influence the career plans of youth, increasing their interest in attending medical schools. MedQUEST provides an educational model that other communities can consider. On a smaller scale, community leaders can also organize healthcare-related career fairs and ask healthcare professionals to make classroom presentations in rural high schools.

SUMMARY

Successful recruitment of healthcare professionals requires a multi-pronged approach. Community leaders can offer financial incentives to attract new healthcare professionals. However, the overall attractiveness of the community and its amenities, and opportunities and services available to healthcare professionals' families, are equally important. CED professionals should reinforce the importance of the healthcare sector in economic development planning. Their knowledge of the local economic environment can also inform the design of recruitment strategies to meet current and expected community needs.

11

Attracting New Investments in Rural Communities

Rural areas are often marked by low levels of financial investment, infrastructure, and business and government services. This constrained investment climate is a reflection of the relatively high costs of these services in rural communities, which in turn is often a function of low population densities, low levels of economic development, and the slow penetration of new commercial activities. As a result, rural areas often face decreased productivity and specialization, which in turn further hinders investment opportunities, even though rural areas offer advantages to investors for certain activities, e.g., those that benefit from lower labour and land costs.

RURAL DEVELOPMENT CONSTRAINTS

A number of studies have identified the most significant investment climate and business environment constraints to be infrastructure, business financing availability and cost, and labour force availability and skills.

Infrastructure

Rural areas are characterized by low population density, which makes public services and basic infrastructure costly, and often unaffordable. The result is reduced access to services most attractive to business investors: public utilities such as power, public transportation options and accessible transportation corridors for movement of goods, high-speed telecommunications, water and waste water treatment facilities, and postal services. Between 2000 and 2008, the Canada-Ontario Infrastructure Program (COIP), a federal government initiative in partnership with Ontario's local governments and the private sector, invested $680.7 million to improve urban and rural municipal infrastructure. The goal of this investment was to improve the quality of life for Ontario residents and make a long-term contribution to creating a dynamic and innovative economy. It focused on improving the quality and safety of drinking water; sports, recreation, and cultural facilities; and bridges. In this way, it made a positive impact on rural communities. Rural investors require significant investments in critical infrastructure such as:[1]

- Transportation structures – bridges, roads, rail and transit and navigable waterways and dams
- Drinking water and wastewater treatment facilities
- Public parks and recreation facilities
- Educational infrastructure – primary education, trades, college, and university
- Recycling, waste, and hazardous waste handling facilities

Business Financing Availability and Cost

Often, investors in rural areas provide loans that are relatively small. Given the sometimes low and fluctuating incomes of a dispersed group of borrowers, financiers face high transaction costs for financing rural projects. Hence, rural lending can be costly and risky. Procedures for obtaining loans from informal sources (e.g., other community members) are less rigorous and therefore appealing to many rural borrowers, even though the interest rates they incur may be higher. Studies show that rural enterprises often rely on household savings and the resources of friends and neighbours, both for enterprise start-up costs and to finance their needs for operating capital. For those who access institutional services, the term structure of lending tends to be skewed heavily towards the short term. This limits rural entrepreneurs' ability to leverage funds for current business operations and expansion opportunities.

In addition to promoting traditional approaches for financing new business ideas through formal lending institutions or own-capital financing, economic development (CED) practitioners can encourage rural entrepreneurs to consider three alternatives: micro-credit, venture capital, and angel investments. Understanding the benefits

---

Financing Options for Rural Business
Micro-credit Resources

1 *Canadian Youth Business Foundation (CYBF)* – http://www.cybf.ca
2 *Community Futures Development Corporations* – http://www.ontcfdc.com
3 *Ottawa Community Loan Fund* – http://www.oclf.org
4 *PARO: A Northwestern Ontario Women's Community Loan Fund* – http://www.paro.ca
5 *Two Rivers Community Development Centre (TRCDC)* – http://www.tworivers.ca
6 *Ignite: A Program of the Spark Centre and the Region of Durham* – http://www.ignitedurham.ca/ignite/

Government Sources of Funding
Federal and provincial governments provide loans and grants to businesses. For a comprehensive listing and detailed information, see http://www.grantcanada.com.

---

and risks associated with each option, as well as being familiar with potential sources of finance, will be an asset when counseling new entrepreneurs.

MICRO-CREDIT
An important key to successful rural business development is leveraging micro-financing. "Micro-credit" can be defined as small loans made to individuals to undertake self-employment or start small businesses. This type of financing is available from a number of different sources, including independent non-profit organizations, community economic development programs, and commercial financial institutions. Often, a micro-credit lender serves a particular geographic area or community. The loans typically are small (e.g., under $25,000) and for entrepreneurs who have not been able to secure financing through traditional lenders. Loans can be provided along with technical support such as business training, mentoring, peer exchanges, and/or networking opportunities.

Rural businesses can take advantage of these loans to cover start-up costs (e.g., land, buildings, fixtures, equipment, supplies, vehicles, pre-opening expenses, and opening inventory) and day-to-day operating costs (e.g., inventory, payroll, rent, taxes, and advertising). The Canada-Ontario Business Service Centre provides micro-credit financing from a number of different sources. A successful rural enterprise may make use of several sources of finance.

VENTURE CAPITAL

Venture capitalists are companies or individuals who provide investment capital, management expertise, and experience. Venture capital often comes from a group of wealthy investors, investment banks, and/or other financial institutions. In return for investment, venture capitalists will take an equity position in the company being supported, usually in proportion to the amount of their investment and the level of risk involved. The future return on their investment is tied to the performance of the company.

Veikko Thiele confirms in his study on venture capital financing for entrepreneurs in rural businesses[2] that venture capital is an important source of start-up financing, particularly for risky ventures with high growth potential. He notes, however, that a high reliance on external financing, combined with a vulnerability to market uncertainties, can affect the long-run performance and even the survival of rural enterprises.

The nature of the venture capital market poses non-trivial challenges for rural entrepreneurs. First, the venture capital market is cyclical and may not be responsive (available) during times of economic uncertainty. Additionally, start-ups in rural communities are often considered low-growth investments and therefore less suitable for venture capital. Secondly, investments are often clustered geographically to take advantage of networks among entrepreneurs. These clusters are less likely to exist in rural communities.

Thiele's study provides two key recommendations to increase access to venture capital funds and improve the survival rate of business ventures in rural areas: (1) Seek to establish publicly-funded venture capital funds with a mandate to only invest in regions where local entrepreneurs have limited access to private venture capital. (2) Establish programs that assist entrepreneurs in objectively evaluating the potential of their business models and preparing professional business plans that specifically cater to venture capitalists. The first of these recommendations is intended for consideration in policy development by provincial and federal governments. The

---

Angel Investors and Venture Capitalist Resources
Angel Investors
  http://www.angelinvestor.ca
  http://www.angelforum.org
  http://www.angelinvestmentnetwork.net
  http://www.ventureworthy.com
  http://www.businessplanmaster.com
Venture Capitalists
  http://www.aprilis.com
  http://www.fundingpost.com

---

second recommendation outlines steps that CED practitioners can take to support entrepreneurs in rural communities.

ANGEL INVESTORS

An angel investor is a person who invests in a business venture, providing capital for start-up or expansion. The investor usually is looking for a higher rate of return than would be gained from a more traditional investment (e.g., 25 per cent or more). The angel investor is often looking for a personal opportunity as well as an investment and will want to play a role in mentoring and managing the company. Organizations like the National Angel Capital Organization (http://nacocanada.com) and the Angel One Investor Network (http://www.angelonenetwork.ca) connect entrepreneurs directly with investors, venture capitalists, and business funds.[3]

Labour Force Availability and Skills

As discussed more fully in Chapter 7, rural areas often have few or no post-secondary education institutions in their communities, limited access to adult education or skills upgrading courses, and few local on-the-job, or other, training opportunities. These factors limit the development of skills and capacities required for economic development. Although labour skills have consistently been shown to be a key determinant in attracting investment, the wide dispersion of rural populations makes establishing viable training institutions and programs a challenge. Funding from the Manitoba and federal

Mobile Training Labs – Red River College (RRC)

Red River College's tagline, "Going Places," is now more true than ever thanks to an innovative new program that brings trades training directly to rural and northern communities. RRC's two new mobile training labs are the backbone of this training initiative to deliver quality applied learning throughout Manitoba. Each lab consists of a fifty-three-foot trailer with pop-out sides that can quickly transform into a 950 ft2 training facility. Diesel generators supply the necessary power to operate electrical equipment, as well as lighting, heating, and air conditioning. Supply trailers can connect to the mobile lab, increasing the total facility space to almost 2,000 ft2. The portability of the training labs allows the College to deliver nationally-recognized trades training wherever it is needed in subjects such as automotive services, carpentry, electrical services, machining, pipe fitting, plumbing, welding, and industrial mechanics. The labs increase accessibility for students in rural areas to training programs, and link training with community-based projects and emerging industries. It allows students to remain at home to study, connects with community supports, and helps build labour capacity in rural and aboriginal communities.

governments, however, has brought about an innovative solution in a number of communities.

The Red River College mobile training lab is a portable trades training institute run out of a 53-foot trailer that moves between communities. When linked to supply trailers, the mobile lab provides 2,000 ft^2 of training space. Funded by $3.12 million in grants, this project brings automotive service, carpentry, electrical, plumbing, and other trades training to rural Manitobans.

CREATIVE ECONOMY INFRASTRUCTURE INVESTMENTS

Richard Florida, author of *The Rise of the Creative Class*, has identified creativity as a driving force of economic growth. Creative industries and activities such as the performing arts, museums and heritage and entertainment industries, literary publishing, architecture and design, and visual arts and crafts play important roles in economic development. This is described more fully in Chapter 6. Today, many rural community leaders are attempting to attract investments to support the creative economy.

Investments in creative economy infrastructure when combined with skills training can offer significant returns. A recent example of this expanded impact is a federal investment in Eastern Ontario's first 3D/HD training centre for television content and the creation of a 3D Film and Editing Technology Centre of Excellence in Prince Edward County. The Headland New Media Development Organization in partnership with WhistleStop Productions Inc. and Loyalist College partnered to deliver a Post-Diploma Certificate in 3D Video Production to post-graduate students in the television and new media industry. The program is currently based in the Headland Incubator, an innovative facility supporting multimedia start-up companies. This investment stimulates immediate job creation and provides training for innovative and cutting-edge jobs of the future while building the skills base and capacity of the community. New employment opportunities arise as graduates create programming for domestic and international television markets, and discover opportunities to launch entrepreneurial ventures within a rural context. Ultimately, the impact will expand beyond movies and games to applications in healthcare, architecture and design, multiplying the original investments many times over.[4]

SUMMARY

While rural areas offer some business advantages, the lower populations and resultant higher costs for infrastructure and services can be barriers to new investment. CED practitioners have important roles to play in brokering the assets associated with rural areas to prospective new business investors and in helping rural entrepreneurs access micro-credit, venture capital, and/or angel investments. Understanding the benefits and risks associated with traditional lending institutions and with each alternative funding source helps enable them to coach and support new entrepreneurs effectively. They can assist with the review and fine tuning of business plans before they are presented to potential investors.

CED practitioners can also innovatively address labour market limitations and build creative economy infrastructure to assist municipalities in their efforts to attract both entrepreneurs and investors.

Fast Facts

Business: WhistleStop Productions

http://www.whistlestoptv.com

Location: Picton, Prince Edward County, Ontario

Key Products: Sports-based television production, custom programming, documentaries and corporate video production

Success Factors:

- High value position
- Niche branding
- Reputation and industry profile

Potential for Growth:

- Utilization of Internet components to add to current offerings
- Online advertising
- HD documentaries

Case Study – WhistleStop Productions

Company Overview and Background

WhistleStop Productions produces high-quality programming for network television. In the 1980s, David Hatch was working in Toronto, the epicentre of Canada's media industry. After starting out as an audio engineer, David went on to support the launch of The Sports Network (TSN), and then moved into daily news reporting for Global Television. In 1989, he branched out and founded his own video production company, Whistle-Stop Productions. In 2000 WhistleStop relocated to Bloomfield in Prince Edward County. Their flagship product is *Motorcycle Experience*, a documentary hosted by David. They have also developed more than forty other original television series.

In addition to sports-based television series, WhistleStop develops custom programming for a range of clients. This ranges from documentaries to custom corporate videos. WhistleStop has invested in the newest HD production equipment and while they are a small firm, their equipment matches or exceeds even their largest competitors' standards.

Industry Overview

One major driver of business for WhistleStop is federal legislation regulated by the Canadian Radio-television Telecommunications Commission (CRTC). The CRTC requires that Canadian networks broadcast a certain percentage of Canadian content. This means that both networks, such as TSN, and providers, such as Bell ExpressVu, are continually seeking Canadian-based programming, thus bolstering enterprising Canadian production houses.

WhistleStop does operate, however, in a highly competitive, price-sensitive market. While their low overhead allows them to price competitively, their clients have grown to expect low prices from the firm and the majority of the company's projects make limited contributions to the bottom line. Given the competitive landscape, it is difficult for the firm to raise prices, as clients have increased bargaining power and can easily replace Whistle-Stop with a competitor.

To be profitable, WhistleStop follows the industry-wide practice of integrating product placement into their shows. It aims to leverage this strength and its existing sponsor relationships to drive additional revenue, potentially through website expansion.

The industry largely depends on a broadcaster distribution method of selling shows to television channels. Accordingly, while large networks are small production houses' largest clients, they are also competitors in that they already have the resources to produce profitable shows in-house. These business partners are thus a threat as they can poach shows and sponsors.

Success Factors

WhistleStop Productions has succeeded where many of its competitors have failed. A number of key success factors have contributed to its growth:

1 High Value Position

WhistleStop has positioned itself as a premier HD video content producer while maintaining competitive pricing, a strategy that drives the business. WhistleStop has leveraged their reduced living costs to enable them to purchase state-of-the-art equipment. By owning comprehensive recording, mixing, and editing equipment, every single aspect of the production process is controlled in-house. The company has been able to reduce traditional variable costs including equipment rental through the fixed purchase of all their equipment.

2 Niche Branding

As a niche player in the video production industry, WhistleStop has been able to offer high-quality, revenue-generating, alternative sports programming. The crown jewel of its portfolio is *Motorcycle Experience*. Whistle-Stop is the sole owner of this program which showcases the motorcycle culture. The program includes test drives, interviews of prominent figures in the sport, and lifestyle pieces, all drawn together by David's charismatic hosting. *Motorcycle Experience* is very popular among bike enthusiasts and moderate bikers reaching 110,000 viewers, a significant figure given the Canadian motorcycle demographic lies around the 100,000 mark. With that exposure in mind, WhistleStop has been able to generate significant profit from manufacturer sponsorships and product placement. Each segment now has an individual sponsor and the overall program is sponsored by Toyota. The incorporation of product placement into the show is very lucrative because brands are promoted as part of the lifestyle without requiring direct promotion. These product placements generate about four times the revenue of paid commercials.

3 Reputation and Industry Profile

With the popularity of the *Motorcycle Experience*, WhistleStop has been able to pursue vanity projects in the documentary sector to showcase its production expertise. Although these projects do not generate a profit, they reinforce the quality of WhistleStop's products in the industry. These documentaries include guitar and mountain climbing pieces that appeal to niche lifestyles. Through these products, WhistleStop maintains its profile in the broadcast industry, thus attracting potential clients.

4 Strategic Opportunities

Given its strengths, WhistleStop possesses several growth opportunities. Expanding *Motorcycle Experience* with an online component would build on a number of strategic advantages. These include a community dedicated to the content of the show, additional video material connected to the weekly episodes, and blogs. First, the generated metrics from online activity would prove valuable in terms of negotiating the price for future shows, thereby increasing their margins. Second, additional sources of revenue could be gained through the exposure of online advertisements to the highly engaged customer group. Third, the investment and experience with online activity could provide a model for future productions, such as HD documentaries. This would give the company an opportunity to increase the attractiveness of future shows and provide an advantage in terms of pricing and negotiations.

Lessons Learned

WhistleStop has invested in the newest technologies to gain a competitive edge in their industry. In addition, WhistleStop strives to be a lean operation. Streamlining operations to reduce costs can help create a winning company and be achieved in many ways including utilizing new procedures, technologies, and locations. WhistleStop has also benefited from multiple revenue streams. Finally, WhistleStop has demonstrated the importance of showcasing specific organization skills and successes in order to market their expertise to potential customers. It has creatively used past successes and a loyal customer base to generate new successes.

12

Goods, Services, and People Movement

Rural transportation systems can increase accessibility to essential services, make travel easier, and increase the quality of life for citizens. Transportation systems can lead to lower commuting costs for residents, thereby increasing intercity travel and fostering the development of local and regional businesses.

ISSUES WITH RURAL TRANSPORTATION

In order to create effective transportation models for an increasingly aging population, rural community leaders must address key challenges and be aware of the significant economic impacts of public transit.

Challenges

Senior citizens use public transit more than any other age group in Canada. Researchers estimate that Canadians sixty-five or older will make up approximately 25 per cent of Canada's population by 2031.[1] In addition, young Canadians between the ages of twenty and forty-four tend to live in large urban centres, as opposed to rural communities.[2] This increases further the proportion of senior citizens in rural communities. Two significant challenges in rural mobility for Eastern Ontario and Western Quebec are residents' access to healthcare, and the fact that many elderly citizens are unable to drive.[3] Rural public transportation is also important for disabled Canadians and low-income families.

Healthcare is an essential service. Personal automobiles are used in many rural communities, obviating the need for public transportation for medical purposes. However, many senior citizens do not drive. For them, the lack of transportation can severely restrict everyday activities such as visiting hospitals and pharmacies, keeping doctor and dentist appointments, visiting friends and family, and shopping for groceries. For the elderly, public transportation is an important service, but in rural areas, it can be quite expensive.

Kings Transit Authority in Nova Scotia uses buses to transport rural citizens back and forth in five different rural communities: Wolfville, Kentville, Berwick, Kings County, and Brooklyn. These communities are challenged by the number of elderly people in need of transportation, yet unable to drive. Public transportation to these communities makes personal travel much easier and increases the viability of small business. However, there are public transportation system challenges. These include a lack of sidewalks in rural Nova Scotia, large amounts of snow in the winter, higher fares as compared with urban transportation, higher speed limits on rural roads, and inconvenience for residents using wheelchairs where bus stops may be a long distance away.

In some communities, a drawback to implementing a rural transportation system can be the reluctance to change. Rural residents may not be supportive of changed transportation modes immediately; often a three-year investment is needed to effectively implement a new program.[4]

Government relations and policies can present further challenges to rural transportation initiatives. The processes and steps to be followed can be very complex. Often the municipal government must first request funding for a rural transportation project. The amount of red tape may increase with the size of the municipality, so it may be more difficult for larger municipalities with more formal government structures to proceed, since more stakeholders are affected and there is more bureaucracy.[5] After this, approval may need to be requested from the regional government, involving another extensive application process. The US supports rural transportation at a federal level, while in Canada it is mostly a provincial mandate.[6] The Canadian Urban Transit Association (CUTA) has actively pursued federal funding for public transportation initiatives, and Infrastructure Canada's Public Transportation Fund has supported several rural communities in British Columbia and Nova Scotia. In cases where rural communities have one major employer, municipalities can partner with employers to create special transportation programs. Rabbit Transit in York, Pennsylvania has used this approach with the regional hospital.[7]

Financial barriers also exist when implementing rural transpor-· tation models, since it can be difficult to justify a transportation system that carries a small number of passengers over large distances.[8] The 2003 Durham Transportation Master Plan showed that rural communities in the Region of Durham were better off using demand-responsive transit services. These included public paratransit, van pools, school buses, and taxis. This was not surprising due to the low population density and the high operational costs of a full-service bus line.

Economic Impacts of Public Transit in Rural Areas

Public transit in rural areas has economic impacts in at least five major areas: employment and business activity, mobility increases, system user costs, expenditure patterns, and local economy growth. These impacts can be measured after a system has been implemented.

1 EMPLOYMENT AND BUSINESS ACTIVITY

Most Canadians rely on employment as their primary source of income. Difficulties associated with travel to work in rural areas can create obstacles for employees. Public transit systems can lead to increased employment and local business activity.[9] The increased employment can be measured by per capita employment or salary changes. Additional business activity can be monitored, for instance, through changes in the size of the business and its revenues. Increased business activity can result partly from increased access by, and revenues from, non-local customers.

2 INCREASED MOBILITY

The ability to access education and training programs can drastically increase citizens' long-term employment prospects.[10] Increased mobility can also help rural residents continue living independently, with access to essential services such as healthcare, post offices, and grocery stores. Mobility can be monitored by the number and frequency of riders in the rural community.

Rural Community Transit Systems
Deseronto Transit – Deseronto, Ontario
http://deseronto.ca/departments/deseronto-transit
Deseronto's transit system provides services to Deseronto, Belleville, Napanee, and Prince Edward County. It operates from Monday to Saturday and uses small buses to serve rural communities.
Green Rider – Hantsport, Nova Scotia
http://www.greenrider.ca
This vanpool service has been running since 1981 and offers rural residents along a commonly travelled route the opportunity to schedule rides to work and school. The service also transports people to Halifax and Dartmouth.
Kings Transit – Berwick, Kentville, Wolfville, and County of Kings, Nova Scotia
http://www.kingstransit.ns.ca
This rural public bus system was established in 1981 and serves the above county and towns, who jointly fund the service. In September 2007, the service was expanded to serve Hants County and parts of Annapolis County.
Kootenay Rideshare – Nelson, British Columbia
http://www.kootenayrideshare.com
This free service helps connect rural residents who wish to share cars and save costs. The website includes emissions calculators and helps individuals to form ridesharing groups.
Ottawa's Rural Routes, OC Transpo – Ottawa, Ontario
http://www.octranspo1.com/riding-with-oc-transpo/rural_partner_routes/
OC Transpo introduced service to rural communities in 2002, and now serves 13 small communities in the greater Ottawa area. The buses operate during peak hours.
Specialized Transit – Prince Edward County, Ontario
http://www.pecounty.on.ca/government/rec_parks_culture/properties/transit.php
This specialized transit system was developed in 2007 for elderly and disabled citizens. Riders must be eligible. Registration involves an application process. Trips are scheduled at least one day in advance and serve social and health needs.

Trius Transit – Charlottetown, Prince Edward Island
http://www.triustransit.ca
This public bus system started in 2005 and serves Charlottetown, Cornwall, Stratford, and some county lines. Ridership
for the transit system continues to grow and revenues from
transit fares offset system costs.

3 TRANSPORTATION COST IMPACTS FOR SYSTEM USERS
Rural transportation can be much less expensive per traveller than
other modes of transportation such as taxi service or friends with
vehicles.[11] Cost savings of public transportation can be measured
and compared to a baseline. Demonstrated reductions in costs
can lead to healthier transportation system budgets and improved
services.

4 IMPACTS ON EXPENDITURE PATTERNS
Travelling to larger urban centres or other rural communities via
public transit can decrease the cost of travel. However, the net economic cost (for the local economy) may not decrease if local residents use the transportation system extensively to purchase lower
priced services and products from non-local merchants.[12]

5 GROWTH IMPACTS ON THE LOCAL ECONOMY
Property in rural areas is generally less expensive, so operating costs
like parking are generally lower than in urban areas. Traffic con-
gestion and accidents also tend to be less likely. Public transit can
offer tourists and visitors an affordable way to visit rural communities and, as mentioned, support small and medium-sized businesses.
Rural property value also has the potential to increase with stable
rural public transit systems in place.[13]

These five economic impact areas may be included in an Economic Impact Analysis (EIA) when introducing a new rural public
transit system. An EIA may be developed to examine the effects of a
potential or existing transit system. This may be useful for general
community knowledge, advocacy for funding, and testing the feasibility of a project.

Canada's Vision for Rural Transportation

Canada's population is expected to rise beyond 40 million by the year 2040.[14] This has sparked national interest in public transportation initiatives. Specifically, the Vision 2040 initiative by CUTA aims to maximize the contribution of public transportation to quality of life, to develop and support an efficient economy, and to maintain a healthy natural environment. This will be accomplished by increasing service options, centralizing transit within communities, developing a national transit policy, ensuring financial funding is available, and maintaining a focus on customers.

Currently in the US, transportation systems are subsidized, including bus, train, air, and road. This is not the case for Canada, because not all transportation systems are considered *vital community services*.[15]

STRATEGIES FOR RURAL TRANSPORTATION

Developing strategies for rural transportation systems requires understanding the types of sustainable rural public transportation, project evaluation processes, and decision-making tools.

Types of Sustainable Rural Public Transportation

Public transit using buses is present in almost all of Canada's forty-nine urban centres with populations of more than 30,000.[16] Rural communities can use this transportation model; however, operating costs are generally too high for sparsely populated communities. One successful case is Ottawa's rural routes initiative, which offers service to thirteen small communities during peak hours. The additional routes were contracted through Ottawa's OC Transpo to serve a combined rural population of approximately 84,500. Rural passes cost 64 per cent more than regular adult passes.[17] Another successful example is Deseronto Transit, which uses small buses to connect rural communities with small urban centres including Belleville and Napanee.

Charter programs are effective for rural communities with smaller populations. Chartering buses and vans for daily routes can provide residents with an alternate mode of transportation at reduced costs. This type of service can also be contracted with large employers in rural areas. Ride sharing and car sharing are two other popular alternatives. Ride sharing consists of carpooling with other commuters found through websites such as http://www.Carpool.ca and http://www.eRideshare.com. Car sharing involves joining a co-op where many users have the opportunity to pay for shared vehicle use.

Other approaches to public transportation include:

- Active transportation: This method of transportation promotes a healthy lifestyle by promoting cycling, walking, and inline skating, and is useful for small communities.
- Vanpooling, Ride-On programs, and guaranteed ride services: Transportation Management Associations in the US provide such services through partial Federal Government funding.[18]
- Telework programs: Some companies establish remote offices to accommodate rural citizens, reducing the need for public transportation by allowing residents to work from home.
- Transit-Oriented Development (TOD): Community planning can organize new housing and essential services around a public transportation hub, in order to increase ridership and commutability.

Evaluation Processes and Decision-Making Tools

Transportation evaluation models can be used to analyze potential projects. They typically include information on government costs, vehicle operating costs, average travel speeds, crash risk per kilometre, project construction, and environmental impacts.[19] To be comprehensive, they should also include parking, vehicle depreciation, construction project delays, land use impacts, and public health considerations.

Developing an *economic evaluation* includes quantifying a potential project and comparing different options. To do this requires deciding on the type of evaluation, evaluation criteria, modeling techniques, the base case, and uncertainty.[20] A second important evaluation is that of transit service quality. This separate evaluation defines themes such as availability, price structure, security, frequency, and reliability.[21] All key stakeholders should be involved in developing the transportation system plans and making decisions.[22] The range of stakeholders in rural communities is usually broad, since there typically is no transportation authority in place. Stakeholders may include the local municipal government, schools, hospitals, transportation companies, employers, churches, and rural citizens.[23]

SUMMARY

Rural communities nationwide share a common concern regarding transportation systems and the impact that mobility challenges have on many community sectors. The lack of public transportation systems often leads to depopulation which in turn further restricts future community options. CED practitioners can assist municipalities with the generation of transportation models and their evaluation. Economic development planning should include the analysis of the transportation systems serving the community and the potential for improving access to employment, education and training, social and health services, and recreation.

Conclusion

Much of Canada's potential is fostered or limited by its vast area and rural, often remote, communities. This guide has presented information from a multi-year project on "Revitalizing Rural Economies by Mobilizing Academic Knowledge," led by Dr Yolande Chan, and coordinated by the Monieson Centre at Queen's School of Business, Queen's University. The Centre is committed to promoting Canada's rural economy. This closing section summarizes the book's contributions and points to related initiatives by the Centre and other Canadian organizations to improve the competitiveness of rural communities.

The guide provided an overview of community economic development, pointing out new priorities, valued assets, and trends. The importance of rural Canadians, and the strength and vulnerabilities of their social ties and capital, were highlighted. The guide outlined strategies for providing first-rate social and employment opportunities for rural youth, and attracting new immigrants to rural communities. New economic opportunities were outlined, including those promoting rural entrepreneurship and incubators, the creative economy, tourism regions, revitalized downtowns, skilled trades, and value-added products and services in traditional industries.

This guide also pointed to necessary investments in infrastructure to promote rural communities, especially those that are remote. These investments include traditional transportation systems, and evolving technology infrastructures (e.g., broadband to provide Internet access and global connectivity), as well as social and cultural infrastructures such as healthcare, education, and recreation services. Financing options for rural businesses were outlined. The

---

Queen's Business Consulting

Queen's Business Consulting (QBC) served as a key partner in the Knowledge Impact in Society (KIS) project coordinated by the Monieson Centre. Through project funding and in-kind support from QBC, more than fifteen rural eastern Ontario businesses received free consulting services. QBC helped these small businesses and community organizations identify leading management strategies to address operational challenges.

QBC is one of Canada's top undergraduate consulting programs. Having been in operation for over thirty years, QBC is a year-round venture managed by senior undergraduate commerce students under the direction of Queen's School of Business faculty. Typical projects result in improved productivity, enhanced morale, reduced expenses, increased cash flows, augmented Internet and e-marketing resources, marketing research, new sources of revenues, increased client retention, and/or strengthened brand awareness for the organization or its products and services.

KIS student consulting projects are described on the Monieson Centre's rural economic revitalization portal at http://www. economicrevitalization.ca.

---

book presented several rural eastern Ontario case studies to showcase rural innovation and business success. Numerous references were provided to support additional study of the issues raised.

The Monieson Centre is committed to the advancement of rural Canada. A number of related research initiatives are outlined at http://business.queensu.ca/centres/monieson.

In 2013, three projects were underway that built directly on the "Revitalizing Rural Economies by Mobilizing Academic Knowledge" (KIS) Project. They are described below. The first of these is the *French Translation of 'Revitalizing Rural Economies by Mobilizing Academic Knowledge' Project*. This project, funded by the Social Sciences and Humanities Research Council of Canada (SSHRC), made available excerpts from this guide to French-speaking readers. Lead partners include the Réseau de Développement Économique et d'Employabilité Ontario, Prince Edward/Lennox & Addington

(PELA) CFDC, and Northumberland County Economic Development & Tourism. For French language materials, contact the authors or the Centre, or visit http://business.queensu.ca/centres/monieson/ revitalisation_economique.

A second related SSHRC-funded project is the *Research Partnerships to Revitalize Rural Economies Project*. This 2011–14 initiative strengthened existing, and developed new, Monieson Centre partnerships with a rural Canada focus. Approximately fifteen researchers at Queen's University, the University of Guelph, the University of Lethbridge, Wilfrid Laurier University, and the Martin Prosperity Institute collaborated. The primary research themes were: Rural Knowledge Workers and Entrepreneurs, and Innovation and Sustainability in Creative Rural Communities. A committed leadership team and steering committee, along with more than 40 partners, guided this research.

A third multi-year project, funded by the Rural Secretariat, focused on assessing *The Impact of Knowledge Mobilization on Rural Economic Development*. Workshops, interviews, and surveys were used by Monieson Centre researchers and staff to assess the extent to and ways in which academic knowledge had contributed to the vitality of rural communities in Southern Ontario. In partnership with the Rural Ontario Institute, RDÉE Ontario, PELA CFDC, and Northumberland County Economic Development & Tourism, the Centre examined the effects of past academic research – such as the Knowledge Impact in Society (KIS) study – on rural development. It documented approaches that were viewed as successful from the perspective of key community, government, business, and academic stakeholders. It also identified new information, tools, and action needed to revitalize rural regions.

The Monieson Centre is privileged to partner with many outstanding organizations with a rural mandate. These include the Ontario Ministry of Rural Affairs; the Rural Ontario Institute; the Prince Edward/Lennox & Addington Institute for Rural Development; the Eastern Ontario CFDC Network, Inc.; and countless others committed to utilizing research to revitalize Canada's rural economies. Other notable research networks and organizations, too, are contributing to rural development in Canada, including the Canadian Rural Research Network, the Canadian Rural Revitalization Federation, the Rural Development Institute, the Alberta Rural Development Network, and the Alberta Centre for Sustainable Rural

Communities. The Monieson Centre is pleased to participate in this vibrant, growing landscape of researchers studying and assisting rural communities.

The book began by outlining economic and social challenges faced by rural communities. It proceeded to outline approaches and strategies to mitigate these challenges. It is a *living document*, shaped by the many Monieson Centre projects and partners outlined above. Readers are encouraged to examine reference materials, the Monieson Centre website, and key partner websites. Canada, without its rural regions, would be a significantly smaller and weaker country. As we work together to strengthen rural communities, we build a more resilient Canada and vibrant world.

Acknowledgments

The authors wish to thank all those who supported the development of this guide from conception to release. We want to acknowledge and express appreciation for the contributions from our academic partners, community and business leaders, and colleagues in the profession of community economic development. We also gratefully acknowledge the written contributions made by the individuals who researched and authored case studies and knowledge syntheses as part of the Knowledge Impact in Society (KIS) project coordinated by the Monieson Centre. Their contributions have been incorporated into the guide. These individuals are:

Ahmad Bakhshai (WhistleStop Productions Case Study)
Troy Beharry (WhistleStop Productions Case Study)
Chris Bruno (The Green Beaver Case Study)
Donald Burns (Wild Wing Case Study)
Ryan DesRoches (Fifth Town Artisan Cheese Co. Case Study)
Daanish Diwan (Pefferlaw Peat Case Study)
Josh Finkelstein (WhistleStop Productions Case Study)
Scott Graham (Wild Wing Case Study)
Justine Habkirk (Fifth Town Artisan Cheese Co. Case Study)
Heather Hall (Chapter 6)
Christopher Henry (Ontario Water Buffalo Case Study)
Ahmad Iqbal (The Green Beaver Case Study)
Yan Luo (Chapter 11)
Kevin Majkut (Chapter 12)
Andrew Macpherson (Wild Wing Case Study)
Maxwell Mausner (Wild Wing Case Study)

Aleksandra Mielczarek (The Green Beaver Case Study)
Kurt Moddemann (Wild Wing Case Study)
Leo Narynskyyi (Pefferlaw Peat Case Study)
Joanna Pleta (The Green Beaver Case Study)
Michael Portner-Gartke (Ontario Water Buffalo Case Study)
Martin Pyle (Chapters 2, 7)
Amanda Reid (Fifth Town Artisan Cheese Co. Case Study)
Matthew Richardson (The Green Beaver Case Study)
Lindsay Robinson (Fifth Town Artisan Cheese Co. Case Study)
Cameron Roblin (Pefferlaw Peat Case Study)
Alexander Russo (WhistleStop Productions Case Study)
Rock Sfeir (Pefferlaw Peat Case Study)
Andrew Smith (Chapter 8)
Courtney Smith (Ontario Water Buffalo Case Study)
Matthew Stam (Pefferlaw Peat Case Study)
Abd-Elhamid Taha (Chapter 9)
Mark Tallon (Wild Wing Case Study)
Johnny Tancredi (Pefferlaw Peat Case Study)
Andrew Tiffin (Ontario Water Buffalo Case Study)
Emilie Timmerman (WhistleStop Productions Case Study)
Rosemary Waldmeier (Ontario Water Buffalo Case Study)
Trevor West (WhistleStop Productions Case Study)
Stephanie Whittamore (Ontario Water Buffalo Case Study)
Arthur Wong (The Green Beaver Case Study)
Ian Wong (Chapters 2, 4, 5, 6, 10)
Jeff Wylie (Chapters 1, 5, 7)
Mengfei Zhou (Fifth Town Artisan Cheese Co. Case Study)
Rachel Zimmer (Ontario Water Buffalo Case Study)

We would also like to thank those who generously provided funding for the research described in this guide and its publication – the Social Sciences and Humanities Research Council of Canada; the Office of Research Services, Queen's University; Queen's School of Business; the Ontario Ministry of Rural Affairs; and the Prince Edward/Lennox & Addington Community Futures Development Corporation.

APPENDICES

Detailed Asset Inventory Categories[1]

The following list outlines the type of information that can be collected for each asset inventory category:

INDIVIDUAL CAPACITIES

1 Community Leaders
- Personal Information
- Community Skills
- Enterprising Interests
- Affiliation in various community groups

HUMAN CAPITAL (INCLUDING K–12 AND HIGHER EDUCATIONAL INSTITUTIONS)

2 K–12 Education Systems
- Number, names, and location of school districts
- Names and contact info of school district leaders
- Number, names, and location of schools
- Names and contact information of principals
- Number of students (including English as second language students)
- Special programs, such as internships and advanced placement for high school students
- Articulation agreements with community colleges
3 Community Colleges
- Number, names, and locations
- Names and contact information of officers

- Number of students, with breakdown by relevant categories (such as full/part time)
- List of academic areas/programs relevant to regional initiatives (with enrollments)
- List of specialized programs and faculty
- Collaborations with business community and with regional K–12 schools
- Number of annual graduates

4 Four-Year Colleges and Universities
- Names and locations of each institution
- Names and contact information of relevant officials, such as president, deans, etc.
- Total enrollments and enrollments in undergraduate and graduate degree programs relevant to regional economic initiatives
- List of specialized programs and faculty
- List of Professional Science Master Degree programs at regional institutions
- List of special purpose facilities
- List of relevant research programs
- Collaborations with regional business community and other institutions that support regional growth
- Number of international students and programs
- Number of online courses offered

5 Private/Non-Profit Technical Schools and Institutes
- Names, location, and contact info for relevant officials
- Areas of specialization
- List of programs
- Affiliations with other area institutions
- Eligibility requirements
- Total enrollment and enrollment in relevant programs

6 Continuing and Professional Education Providers
- Names, location, and contact information for relevant officials
- Nature of institution (e.g., four-year college)
- List of certificates and programs offered
- Affiliations with other regional institutions

7 Available Workforce
- Breakdown of regional population by age groups, including number of adults over 18 years of age
- Location of population within region